CAMBRIDGE
UNIVERSITY PRESS

Cambridge Global English

LEARNER'S BOOK 8

Chris Barker & Libby Mitchell

Contents

Contents

	Use of English	Cross-curricular links	Vocabulary	21st-century skills
	Comparatives and superlatives of adjectives Demonstrative, indefinite and quantitative pronouns Comparatives and superlatives of adverbs Comparative adverb structures Multi-word verbs	Science Biology	Geographical features Wildlife	Learning to learn: Do some research to find out more about a scientific process; give a presentation called 'Why is the sky blue?' Social responsibility: Give advice to a new student Critical thinking: Review what you have learned and talk about what particularly interests you; write a scene to continue a narrative Creative thinking: Write questions for a multiple-choice quiz Collaborative working: Pair work, group work, projects
	Past continuous Verbs followed by prepositions Past perfect simple Past perfect in reported speech	History	Leaders, rulers and explorers Artists, musicians and writers	Learning to learn: Use subject-specific vocabulary to discuss a figure from history; find out about the people from a period of history who are remembered today Social responsibility: Understand how leaders, rulers and explorers contribute to society Critical thinking: Compare historical figures and their achievements Creative thinking: Role-play an interview about who will be remembered in 50 years' time Collaborative working: Pair work, group work, projects
	Present perfect with indefinite time adverbs Present perfect continuous Preposition + noun Reported speech: questions and statements	Literature	Types of story, opinions of stories Useful words and phrases for telling a story	Learning to learn: Understand the concept of genre in storytelling; practise adding detail and variety to a narrative description Social responsibility: Appreciate traditions of storytelling from different cultures Critical thinking: Analyse the appeal of stories and storytelling; summarise a story Creative thinking: Write a story by adapting an original Collaborative working: Pair work, group work, projects
	Use the correct verb tense *what* (= 'the thing(s) which') Participle clauses Questions	Music Statistics	Genres of music Types of music, instruments, performers	Learning to learn: Understand the concept of genre in music; learn to correct mistakes as you are speaking Social responsibility: Appreciate the music of other cultures; understand the part music can play in everyone's life and in particular in the lives of people with disabilities Critical thinking: Identify inconsistencies in what people say; identify implied meaning Creative thinking: Compare and analyse three pieces of music Collaborative working: Pair work, group work, projects

How to use this book

In this book you will find lots of different features to help your learning.

What you will learn in the unit or lesson.

In this unit you will...

- **talk** about languages and learning languages
- **find out** about languages spoken in Papua New Guinea
- **listen** to and **give** opinions about learning languages

Big questions to find out what you know already.

Getting started

" How many languages can you name? Where are they spoken? "

Important words for each unit. These words are included on wordlists in the Teacher's Resource.

a lively neighbourhood	a shopping centre	an apartment block
car-free	green spaces	narrow streets
overlooking the water	traffic congestion	raised walkways

The key words feature includes vocabulary from other subjects.

Key words: Geography and languages

community
creole
independent
pidgin
population

Read real texts with helpful glossaries.

[2] apparently: used to say that you've read or been told something but you're not sure it's true
[7] capable: able to do something
[15] threaten: to be likely to harm or destroy something

Use of English boxes and accompanying questions present the main grammar points in a unit.

Use of English *-ing* forms as subjects and objects

subject
Speaking *to someone in their own language, even if it is only for a short time, makes that person feel more at ease.*

object
*I really enjoy **watching** French TV series.*

A brief revision of other language points.

Remember
How to report commands

(The sorcerer to Aladdin:) 'Give the gold coins to your mother.'

The sorcerer told Aladdin ***to give*** *the gold coins to* ***his*** *mother.*

'Don't lose the ring.'

He told him ***not to lose*** *the ring.*

Strategies you can use to help you with your learning.

Language tip

noun	adjective
cone	conical
sphere	spherical
cylinder	cylindrical

Questions to help you think about how you learn.

- Was it helpful to organise your ideas in four sections: gestures, silence, touch and eye contact?
- Did you include abstract nouns and some short phrases, such as *of course, for example, even if*?

Questions that cover what you have learned in each unit. If you can answer these, you are ready to move on to the next unit.

Check your progress

General knowledge quiz

How much do you remember about what you've learned?

1 Which is the odd one out, and why?

French Japanese Canadian Spanish

2 If someone is bilingual, what does it mean?

3 Match the labels to the numbers on the map.

- Australia

This is what you have learned in the unit.

Summary checklist

I can

- [ ] ask and answer questions about learning languages.
- [ ] discuss the advantages of learning languages.
- [ ] identify the meaning of emojis and discuss the advantages and disadvantages of using them.
- [ ] understand a text about body language in different cultures.
- [ ] discuss what people need to know about body language in our culture.
- [ ] use English idioms in conversation.
- [ ] write a letter about my experience of learning languages to send to an exchange school.
- [ ] write a guide to non-verbal communication in our country.
- [ ] teach my classmates a few words and phrases of a new language.

Audio is available with the Digital Learner's Book, Teacher's Resource or Digital Classroom.

Video is available with Digital Classroom.

Lessons 1 and 4: The **Think about it** lessons introduce topic vocabulary.

Engage with the topic of the unit and generate discussion using the image, the video and the big question.

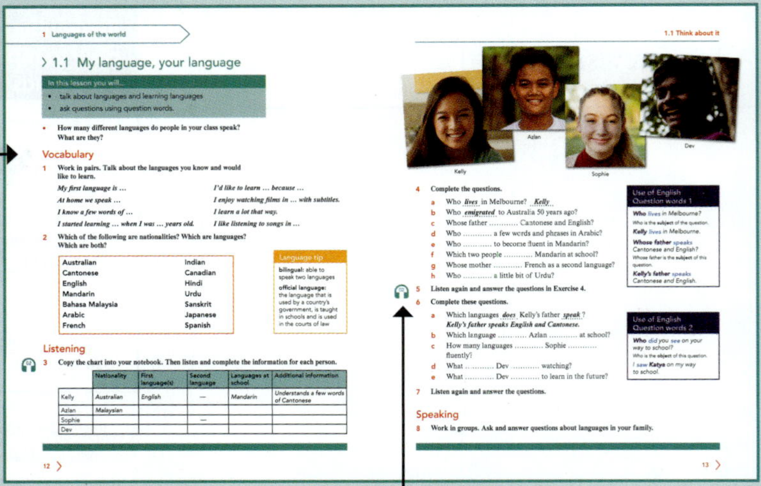

These lessons include listening activities.

Lessons 2 and 5: The **cross-curricular** lessons prepare learners to learn in English across the curriculum.

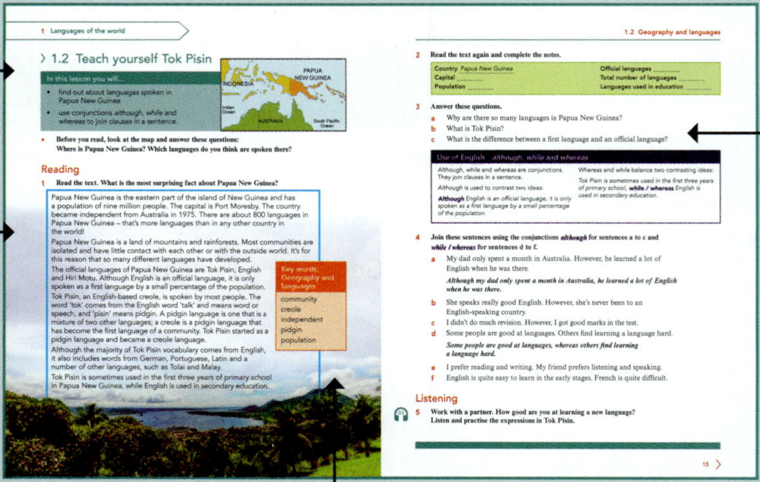

A key text exposes learners to cross-curricular language.

There are opportunities to think critically about the information in the text.

In this lesson you'll find Key words boxes.

Lessons 3 and 6: The **Talk about it** lessons develop learners' speaking skills.

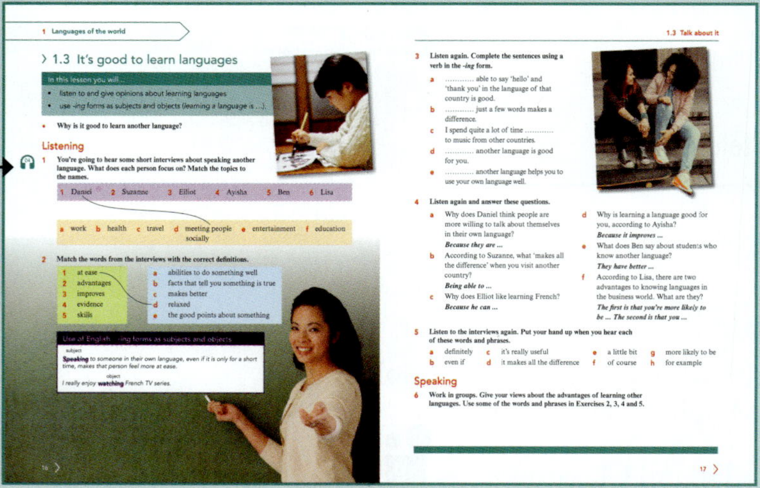

Listening models and speaking tips help provide scaffolding for speaking.

Lesson 7:
The **Write about it** lesson supports learners in writing a variety of text types

Step-by-step tasks support learners in their planning, writing and editing.

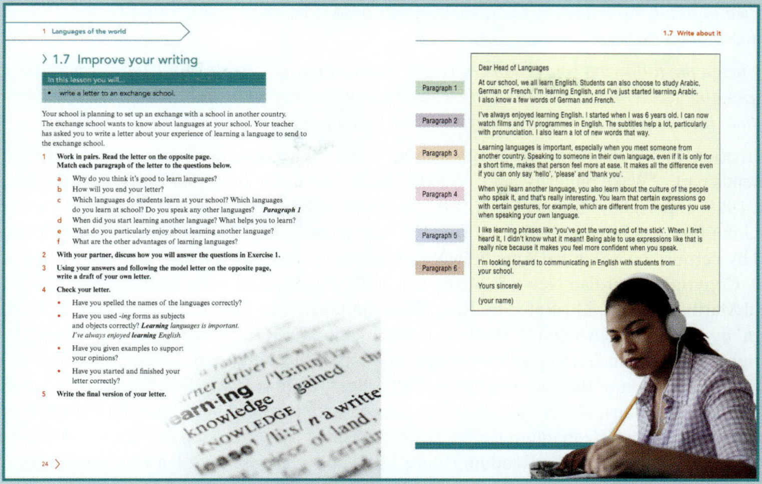

Model texts support the writing process.

Assessment ideas and sample learner answers can be found in the Teacher's Resource.

Lesson 8:
The **Project challenge** lesson provides a choice of projects and an opportunity to consolidate learning from the unit.

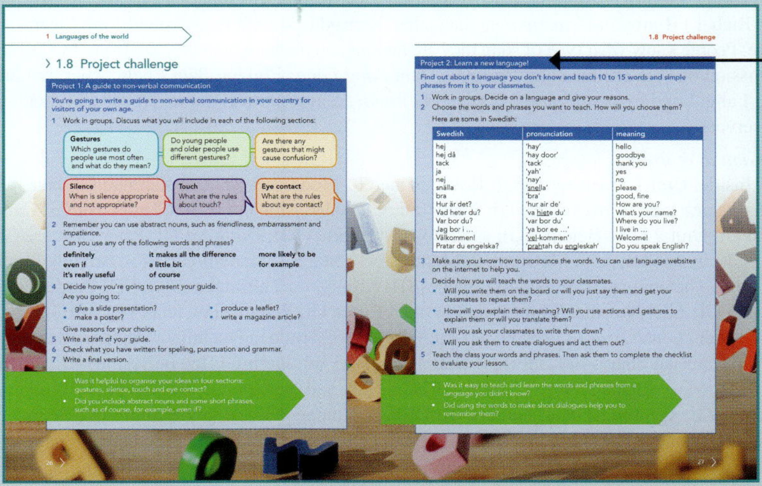

Projects encourage 21st-century skills such as research, collaboration and creativity.

Self- and peer-evaluation checklists for projects are available in the Teacher's Resource.

Lesson 9:
The **Read and respond** lesson is based on authentic texts and includes fiction, non-fiction, poetry and autobiography.

The audio can be played before learners read the text.

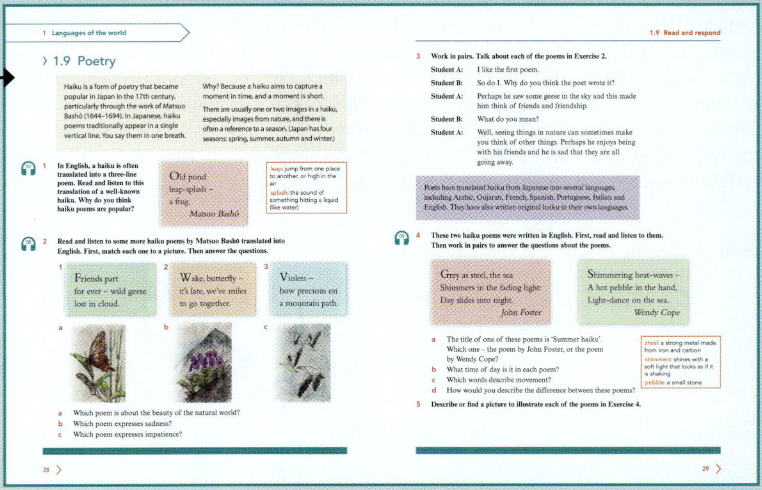

The literature is used as a platform for work on values.

There is also an opportunity for creative writing.

Acknowledgements

The authors and publishers would like to thank the following for reviewing this book: Heather Caroll; Susan Holmes, Nehru World School; and Tim Swihart, Mooltripakdee International School.

The authors and publishers acknowledge the following sources of copyright material and are grateful for the permissions granted. While every effort has been made, it has not always been possible to identify the sources of all the material used, or to trace all copyright holders. If any omissions are brought to our notice, we will be happy to include the appropriate acknowledgements on reprinting.

Unit 1: Excerpt adapted from 'International body language: language with no words' © Telegraph Media Group Limited 2009. Reproduced with permission of *The Telegraph*.; 'Old pond', 'Friends part', 'Wake butterfly' and 'Violets', published in *On Love and Barley: Haiku of Bashoby Matsuo Basho*, translated by Lucien Stryk, Penguin Classics, 1985, copyright © Lucien Stryk, 1985. Reproduced by permission of Penguin Books Ltd; 'Haiku' by John Foster. Reproduced by kind permission of John Foster; 'Summer haiku' by Wendy Cope, from in *The Poetry Store*, Hodder Children's Books, 2005, p.95, copyright © Wendy Cope, 2005. Reproduced by permission of United Agents (www.unitedagents.co.uk) on behalf of Wendy Cope; **Unit 2:** Text adapted from article 'Middle East Eye' 29 January 2019. Copyright Guardian News & Media Ltd 2020. Reproduced with permission of *The Guardian*; *A History of Pictures for Children* by David Hockney and Martin Gayford, illustrated by Rose Blake, published by Thames & Hudson Ltd; **Unit 3:** 'The Doves of Damascus' by Ftoun Abou Kerech, 'The Return' by Maah-Noor Ali and 'I Shall Go Back' by Shukria Rezaei from *England: Poems from a School* by Kate Clanchy. Published by Picador, 2018. Copyright © Kate Clanchy. Reproduced by permission of the author c/o Rogers, Coleridge & White Ltd, 20 Powis Mews, London W11 1JN and reproduced with permission of the Licensor through PLSclear; **Unit 4:** Campaign poster reproduced with permission of SANCCOB; Advert reproduced with permission of Chupa Chups; poster and photo reproduced with permission of Lacoste; **Unit 5:** excerpt from *No One Is Too Small to Make a Difference* by Greta Thunberg, published by Penguin Books 2019. Reprinted by permission of Penguin Books Limited and Penguin Books, an imprint of Penguin Publishing Group, a division of Penguin Random House LLC, all rights reserved; **Unit 6:** Excerpt from 'Live Science article on what causes Bioluminescence' by Benjamin Radford. Reproduced with permission of author; Excerpt from *Why Don't Penguin's Feet Freeze?* by Rick Eraho, © New Scientist, reproduced by permission of John Murray Press, an imprint of Hodder & Stoughton; Excerpt from *The Whale Rider* by Witi Ihimaera, reproduced by permission of Penguin NZ; **Unit 7:** Excerpt from *War Horse* by Michael Morpurgo © 2006, © 1982 by Michael Murpurgo. Reprinted by permission of HarperCollins Publishers Ltd and Scholastic Inc.; **Unit 8:** 'Tidalick' by Pauline E. McLeod, *Gadi Mirrabooka: Australian Aboriginal Tales from the Dreaming*; Helen McKay, editor; Libraries Unlimited; A Division of Greenwood Publishing Group, Inc. https://www.gadimirrabooka.com; **Unit 9:** Excerpt from interview by Richard Bratby in *Gramophone* magazine. Reproduced with permission of the Licensor through PLSclear; Excerpt from 'Music really IS a universal language: People know what type of song they are hearing, no matter where they are from' by Catherine Chapman (freelance writer), MailOnline, reproduced with permission of Solo Syndication; Prologue from *Lang Lang: Playing With Flying Keys* by Lang Lang as told to Michael French, copyright © 2008 by Lang Lang. Used by permission of Delacorte Press, an imprint of Random House Children's Books, a division of Penguin Random House LLC. All rights reserved.

Thanks to the following for permission to reproduce images:
Cover: Ros Roberts/Getty Images; Inside: Unit 1 Smartboy10/GI; Rob Lewine/GI; Mohd Safwan Abd Rahman/GI; pamspix/GI; Shiv Mer/GI; Westend61/GI; Makiko Tanigawa/GI; Jose Luis Pelaez Inc/GI; martin-dm/GI; PhotoTalk/GI; Aslan Alphan/GI; JGI/Tom Grill/GI; Catherine Falls Commercial; Terry Vine/GI; VII-photo/GI; Yagi Studio/GI; Unit 2 Dina Belenko/GI; smartboy10/GI; bruev/GI; DarthArt/GI; Peter Dazeley/GI; Igor Nietkov/GI; stockcam/GI; Sarote Impheng/GI; amriphoto/GI; ilbusca/GI; John McCormick/Shutterstock; Marc Romanelli/GI; Nick Brundle Photography/GI; Stefano Montesi - Corbis/GI (x2); alex grabchilev/evgeniya bananova/GI; Education Images/GI; Kriangkrai Thitimakorn/GI; SDI Productions/GI; asbe/GI; fotofrog; Unit 3 Hiroshi Watanabe/GI; @ Didier Marti/GI; Adel Newman/Shutterstock; Omar Torres/GI; Przemysław Iciak/GI; Jose Luis Pelaez Inc/GI; Marko Takala/GI; ViewStock/GI; Paul Burns/GI; SDI Productions/GI; Jose Luis Pelaez Inc/GI; Sergio Mendoza Hochmann/Shutterstock; enjoynz/GI; PinkyRabbit/GI; John Scott/GI; Tamas Zsebok / EyeEm/GI; Maurian Soares Salvador/GI; Unit 4 © Marco Bottigelli/GI; IconicBestiary/GI; Jinan Liujia Kungfu Needle Shop Advertisement/Trademark Copperplate; Mary Evans Picture Library; API/GI; Daly and Newton/GI; BeylaBalla/GI; Regina Gerum/GI; Mark_KA/GI; Chris Doal/GI; twomeows/GI; Levente Bodo/GI; kgfoto/GI; Paul Souders/GI; DEA/L. Romano/GI; Sergey Ryumin/GI; Bettmann/GI; GraphicaArtis/GI; API/GI; Unit 5 Gandee Vasan/GI; SimonDannhauer/GI; Ondrej Prosicky/GI; Daniel Bosma/GI; mjaud/Shutterstock; leonard_c/GI; Eduardo Ramos Castaneda/GI; alexandrumagurean/GI; StreetFlash/GI; hanabeni/GI; SDI Productions/GI; Sonny Tumbelaka/GI; Brett Hemmings/GI; Tetra Images; Ronald Patrick/GI; Georg Hochmuth/GI; OGphoto/GI; Unit 6 Martin Harvey/GI; Salvatore Virzi/GI; Stocktrek Images/GI; zhengshun tang/GI; Ali Majdfar/GI; Anton Petrus/GI; Westend61/GI; Larry Keller, Lititz Pa./GI; Paul Souders/GI; Boris SV/GI; Roc Canals/GI; William Douglas / EyeEm/GI; Nicola Katie/GI; Vicki Jauron, Babylon and Beyond Photography/GI; Kamil Suchta/GI; Richard I'Anson/GI; Khaichuin Sim/GI; Xavier Leoty/GI; Oliver Strewe/GI; PictureLux/The Hollywood Archive/Alamy Stock Photo; Unit 7 THEPALMER/GI; Dinodia Photos/GI; Print Collector/GI; Interfoto/Alamy Stock Photo; Thomas Imo/GI; DEA Picture Library/GI; Bettmann/GI; Peter Unger/GI; Tibor Bognár/GI; Nick Brundle Photography/GI; DeAgostini/GI; Phil Walter/GI; Hagen Hopkins/GI; Phil Walter/GI; Photo Josse/Leemage/GI; Imagno/GI; Tibor Bognar/GI; Universal History Archive/GI; Stefano Bianchetti/GI; Art Directors & TRIP/Alamy Stock Photo; Miguel Medina/GI; Paolo Bona/Shutterstock; Underwood Archives/GI; Don Cravens/The LIFE Images Collection via Getty Images/GI; Print Collector/GI; bortonia; Ilya S. Savenok/WireImage/GI; alexxx1981/GI; Unit 8 Photo © Isadora/Bridgeman Images; Otto Stadler/GI; LordRunar/GI; Jasmin Merdan/GI (x2); Kech/GI; mrPliskin/GI; Kech/GI; duncan1890/GI; Yuri_Arcurs/GI; ilbusca/GI; bortonia/GI; Horst Mahr/GI; Grant Faint/GI; Tier Und Naturfotografie J und C Sohns/GI; MariaCollado - Pixelgo/GI; Unit 9 Rawf8/GI; studiocasper/GI; John Phillips/GI; Hiroyuki Ito/GI; Thanks to Accessible Arts and Media, an inclusive arts charity in York; Image Source/GI; Andy Sheppard/GI; Thomas Coex/GI; Lightstar59/GI; kzenon/GI; Hiraman/GI; chee gin tan/GI; Iryna Kurolovych/GI; Gustavo Ramirez/GI; Pobytov/GI; Adam Berry/GI; VCG/GI

Key: GI = Getty Images

Music tracks are from Getty Images and Epidemic Sounds via Getty Images

1 Languages of the world

In this unit you will...

- **talk** about languages and learning languages
- **find out** about languages spoken in Papua New Guinea
- **listen** to and **give** opinions about learning languages
- **identify** the meaning of emojis and **discuss** the advantages of using them
- **read** about gestures and other kinds of body language in different cultures
- **learn** some English idioms
- **write** a letter to an exchange school
- **work** together to write a guide to non-verbal communication in your country
- **teach** each other a new language
- **read** haiku poems and **write** a haiku.

Getting started

“How many languages can you name? Where are they spoken?”

Watch this!

1.1 My language, your language

In this lesson you will...

- talk about languages and learning languages
- ask questions using question words.

- **How many different languages do people in your class speak? What are they?**

Vocabulary

1 **Work in pairs. Talk about the languages you know and would like to learn.**

My first language is …

At home we speak …

I know a few words of …

I started learning … when I was … years old.

I'd like to learn … because …

I enjoy watching films in … with subtitles.

I learn a lot that way.

I like listening to songs in …

2 **Which of the following are nationalities? Which are languages? Which are both?**

Australian	Indian
Cantonese	Canadian
English	Hindi
Mandarin	Urdu
Bahasa Malaysia	Sanskrit
Arabic	Japanese
French	Spanish

Language tip

bilingual: able to speak two languages

official language: the language that is used by a country's government, is taught in schools and is used in the courts of law

Listening

02

3 **Copy the chart into your notebook. Then listen and complete the information for each person.**

	Nationality	First language(s)	Second language	Languages at school	Additional information
Kelly	*Australian*	*English*	—	*Mandarin*	*Understands a few words of Cantonese*
Azlan	*Malaysian*				
Sophie			—		
Dev					

Kelly

Azlan

Sophie

Dev

4 **Complete the questions.**

a Who *lives* in Melbourne? *Kelly*
b Who *emigrated* to Australia 50 years ago?
c Whose father .... Cantonese and English?
d Who .... a few words and phrases in Arabic?
e Who .... to become fluent in Mandarin?
f Which two people .... Mandarin at school?
g Whose mother .... French as a second language?
h Who .... a little bit of Urdu?

02 **5** **Listen again and answer the questions in Exercise 4.**

6 **Complete these questions.**

a Which languages *does* Kelly's father *speak*?
Kelly's father speaks English and Cantonese.
b Which language .... Azlan .... at school?
c How many languages .... Sophie .... fluently?
d What .... Dev .... watching?
e What .... Dev .... to learn in the future?

7 **Listen again and answer the questions.**

> **Use of English**
> **Question words 1**
>
> *Who lives in Melbourne?*
> *Who* is the **subject** of the question.
> *Kelly lives in Melbourne.*
> *Whose father speaks Cantonese and English?*
> *Whose father* is the **subject** of this question.
> *Kelly's father speaks Cantonese and English.*

> **Use of English**
> **Question words 2**
>
> *Who did you see on your way to school?*
> *Who* is the **object** of this question.
> *I saw Katya on my way to school.*

Speaking

8 **Work in groups. Ask and answer questions about languages in your family.**

1.2 Teach yourself Tok Pisin

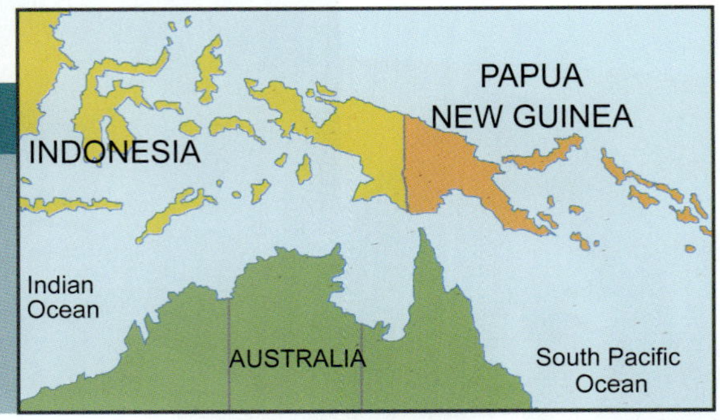

In this lesson you will...

- find out about languages spoken in Papua New Guinea
- use conjunctions *although*, *while* and *whereas* to join clauses in a sentence.

- **Before you read, look at the map and answer these questions:**
  Where is Papua New Guinea? Which languages do you think are spoken there?

Reading

1 **Read the text. What is the most surprising fact about Papua New Guinea?**

Papua New Guinea is the eastern part of the island of New Guinea and has a population of nine million people. The capital is Port Moresby. The country became independent from Australia in 1975. There are about 800 languages in Papua New Guinea – that's more languages than in any other country in the world!

Papua New Guinea is a land of mountains and rainforests. Most communities are isolated and have little contact with each other or with the outside world. It's for this reason that so many different languages have developed.

The official languages of Papua New Guinea are Tok Pisin, English and Hiri Motu. Although English is an official language, it is only spoken as a first language by a small percentage of the population.

Tok Pisin, an English-based creole, is spoken by most people. The word 'tok' comes from the English word 'talk' and means word or speech, and 'pisin' means pidgin. A pidgin language is one that is a mixture of two other languages; a creole is a pidgin language that has become the first language of a community. Tok Pisin started as a pidgin language and became a creole language.

Although the majority of Tok Pisin vocabulary comes from English, it also includes words from German, Portuguese, Latin and a number of other languages, such as Tolai and Malay.

Tok Pisin is sometimes used in the first three years of primary school in Papua New Guinea, while English is used in secondary education.

Key words: Geography and languages

community
creole
independent
pidgin
population

2 **Read the text again and complete the notes.**

Country *Papua New Guinea*	**Official languages** ....
Capital	**Total number of languages** ....
Population	**Languages used in education** ....

3 **Answer these questions.**

- **a** Why are there so many languages in Papua New Guinea?
- **b** What is Tok Pisin?
- **c** What is the difference between a first language and an official language?

Use of English *although, while* and *whereas*

Although, *while* and *whereas* are conjunctions. They join clauses in a sentence.

Although is used to contrast two ideas:

Although *English is an official language, it is only spoken as a first language by a small percentage of the population.*

Whereas and *while* balance two contrasting ideas:

Tok Pisin is sometimes used in the first three years of primary school, ***while / whereas*** *English is used in secondary education.*

4 **Join these sentences using the conjunctions *although* for sentences a to c and *while / whereas* for sentences d to f.**

- **a** My dad only spent a month in Australia. However, he learned a lot of English when he was there.

  Although my dad only spent a month in Australia, he learned a lot of English when he was there.

- **b** She speaks really good English. However, she's never been to an English-speaking country.
- **c** I didn't do much revision. However, I got good marks in the test.
- **d** Some people are good at languages. Others find learning a language hard.

  Some people are good at languages, whereas others find learning a language hard.

- **e** I prefer reading and writing. My friend prefers listening and speaking.
- **f** English is quite easy to learn in the early stages. French is quite difficult.

Listening

03 **5** **Work with a partner. How good are you at learning a new language? Listen and practise the expressions in Tok Pisin.**

1.3 It's good to learn languages

In this lesson you will...

- listen to and give opinions about learning languages
- use *-ing* forms as subjects and objects (*learning a language is …*).

- **Why is it good to learn another language?**

Listening

04

1 You're going to hear some short interviews about speaking another language. What does each person focus on? Match the topics to the names.

1 Daniel 2 Suzanne 3 Elliot 4 Ayisha 5 Ben 6 Lisa

a work b health c travel d meeting people socially e entertainment f education

2 Match the words from the interviews with the correct definitions.

1	at ease	a	abilities to do something well
2	advantages	b	facts that tell you something is true
3	improves	c	makes better
4	evidence	d	relaxed
5	skills	e	the good points about something

Use of English *-ing* **forms as subjects and objects**

subject
Speaking *to someone in their own language, even if it is only for a short time, makes that person feel more at ease.*

object
I really enjoy ***watching*** *French TV series.*

3 **Listen again. Complete the sentences using a verb in the *-ing* form.**

a .... able to say 'hello' and 'thank you' in the language of that country is good.

b .... just a few words makes a difference.

c I spend quite a lot of time .... to music from other countries.

d .... another language is good for you.

e .... another language helps you to use your own language well.

4 **Listen again and answer these questions.**

a Why does Daniel think people are more willing to talk about themselves in their own language?
Because they are ...

b According to Suzanne, what 'makes all the difference' when you visit another country?
Being able to ...

c Why does Elliot like learning French?
Because he can ...

d Why is learning a language good for you, according to Ayisha?
Because it improves ...

e What does Ben say about students who know another language?
They have better ...

f According to Lisa, there are two advantages to knowing languages in the business world. What are they?
The first is that you're more likely to be ... The second is that you ...

5 **Listen to the interviews again. Put your hand up when you hear each of these words and phrases.**

a definitely
b even if
c it's really useful
d it makes all the difference
e a little bit
f of course
g more likely to be
h for example

Speaking

6 **Work in groups. Give your views about the advantages of learning other languages. Use some of the words and phrases in Exercises 2, 3, 4 and 5.**

1.4 Do you speak emoji?

In this lesson you will...

- identify the meaning of emojis and discuss the advantages of using them
- use the present continuous with a variety of verbs.

- **Did you know that more people 'speak' emoji than English? Why do you think this is?**

The word *emoji* comes from the Japanese 'e' meaning 'picture' and 'moji' meaning 'character'.

Vocabulary

1 **Match a description to each emoji.**

emoji

1 

2 

3 

4 

5 

6 

7 

8 

9 

10 

description

a A face with a big smile, eyes in the shape of arches and pink cheeks.

b A face with a big smile, arrow-shaped eyes, crying with laughter, and rolling like a ball.

c A face with a big smile, raised eyebrows, smiling eyes, crying with laughter.

d A face with a big smile, wearing sunglasses.

e A face with eyes closed and three Zs.

f A face with a puzzled look and the thumb and first finger on the chin.

g A face, smiling a little and winking with one eye, usually the left eye.

h A smiling face with red cartoon-style hearts for eyes.

i A cone with party streamers.

j Two hands together pointing upwards.

2 Now match a meaning to each emoji.

a This is a joke. I'm not being serious. *9*

b I'm feeling very sleepy.

c I'm not sure. I'm thinking about it.

d I love this!

e I'm rolling on the floor with laughter.

f I'm feeling happy, warm and positive.

g Please, thank you, I bow to you (*or,* a prayer).

h I'm laughing so much that I'm crying.

i Let's celebrate!

j Cool.

Use of English Present continuous

Remember that we use the present continuous to talk about what is happening at the time of speaking:
I'm ***laughing*** *a lot.*

We also use it to describe how someone is feeling at the time of speaking:
I'm ***feeling*** *very sleepy.*

Some verbs, like *think*, are not normally used in the present continuous. So we say, for example, *I think emojis are very useful*. However, when we talk about something we're doing at the time of speaking, we use the present continuous:
I'm not sure. ***I'm thinking*** *about it.*
NOT I ~~think~~ about it.

You can also use the verb *to be* in the present continuous: ***I'm not being*** *serious.*

3 Use verbs in the present continuous to say what each emoji means.

a Where are you? What are you doing?

I'm sitting on the beach under an umbrella.

b What's the weather like at the moment?

c Do you want to play basketball?

d What's the party like? Are you enjoying it?

e What are you doing at the moment?

Listening

05 **4 Listen to this radio interview with Professor Rory Jones. What is the professor's opinion of emojis? What do you think the presenter's opinion is?**

5 Listen again. What are the advantages of using emojis, according to Professor Jones?

6 Work in groups. Discuss these questions.

a Which are your favourite emojis? Describe them. When do you use them?

b In your opinion, what are the advantages of using emojis? Are there any disadvantages?

c Why do you think emojis have become so widely used?

1.5 Beyond words

In this lesson you will...

- read about gestures and other kinds of body language in different cultures
- use abstract nouns to describe human interaction (*friendliness, confidence, ...*).

Key words: Social studies

body language
culture
eye contact
gesture
non-verbal communication

- **What is non-verbal communication? Can you give some examples?**

Reading

1 **What is the purpose of the magazine article below?**

International body language

A LANGUAGE WITH NO WORDS

Something as simple as a smile can express friendliness in one culture, embarrassment in another and impatience in a third. Even silence means different things in different places.

Language learners spend a lot of time on the vocabulary and grammar of a language, without considering non-verbal communication. Here are four examples of non-verbal communication that vary from culture to culture.

GESTURES The wrong gesture can lead to confusion or offence. Tapping your finger on the side of your head is a gesture that means 'remember' in North America, but suggests madness in Russia. Even nodding 'yes' or shaking one's head for 'no' can be misunderstood. In Turkey, for example, 'no' is expressed by moving the head upwards, whereas in the UK, you move your head from side to side to say 'no'.

SILENCE In North America and the UK, silence can be a problem. At work, at school or with friends, silence can make people feel uncomfortable. However, in other parts of the world, silence is not considered to be negative. In China, for example, silence can be used to show agreement and interest.

TOUCH Much of northern Europe is classed as having 'non-contact' cultures because there's very little physical contact in daily life. Even if you accidentally touch someone's arm, you say 'Sorry!'. By comparison, in the Middle East, Latin America and southern Europe, physical touch is a big part of being with friends and family.

EYE CONTACT In most western countries, eye contact shows that you have confidence in someone and that you are interested in what they are saying. In many Middle Eastern countries, same-gender eye contact is maintained for longer than in the west. In many Asian, African and Latin American countries, however, maintaining eye contact suggests you are angry and aggressive.

Speaking

2 **Work in pairs. Act out each scenario. Respond in the correct way.**

- **a** You're spending your holiday with your Turkish penfriend in Bodrum. Your penfriend asks you if you're hungry and would like something to eat. Make a gesture to say 'No thanks'.
- **b** You're in London and you accidentally bump into someone as you're getting off a bus. What do you say?
- **c** You're on holiday in Mexico. You're visiting the ancient city of Palenque. A guide is showing you round. Do you make eye contact with the guide?

> **Use of English**
> **Abstract nouns**
>
> Remember that we usually use abstract nouns without *the* or *a* / *an*.
>
> *Something as simple as a smile can express* ***friendliness*** *in one culture,* ***embarrassment*** *in another and* ***impatience*** *in a third.*

3 **Find abstract nouns in the article in Exercise 1 to match these adjectives.**

- **a** friendly
- **b** embarrassed
- **c** impatient
- **d** confused
- **e** silent
- **f** confident

4 **Choose an appropriate adjective or abstract noun from Exercise 3 to complete these sentences.**

- **a** Being kind and helpful is a good way of showing *friendliness* .
- **b** Some people are comfortable with .... but others have to talk all the time.
- **c** I'm quite shy, so I feel quite .... if I have to go up to talk at the front of the class.
- **d** There were a lot of people in the room and when the fire alarm went off there was total ....
- **e** You should try not to show .... when people make mistakes.
- **f** When you meet someone for the first time, it gives you .... if they smile at you.

Speaking

5 **Work in groups. Look at the words in the social studies key words box and discuss these questions.**

- **a** What are the main things people need to know about body language in your culture?
- **b** What are the most common gestures in your culture and what do they mean?
- **c** What does a visitor to your country need to know about making eye contact?
- **d** Do you think it's important to know about gestures and communication in other countries and cultures? Why?

1.6 An A to Z of idioms

In this lesson you will...

- learn some English idioms
- write and role-play conversations using idioms.

Language tip

An idiom is a group of words with a meaning that is difficult to guess from the meanings of the separate words. We often use idioms in conversation. They help you to sound more confident and natural, as if you really know the language.

- **If something happens 'once in a blue moon', what do you think this means?**

Reading and listening

1 **Read the A to Z of idioms. Can you guess what some of them mean?**

A It's as easy as ABC.

B It went from bad to worse.

C It was a piece of cake.

D On the dot

E What on earth …?

F You've really put your foot in it.

G It's anybody's guess.

H On the one hand … On the other hand …

I I haven't got the faintest idea!

J It's a good job that …

K I was on a knife-edge.

L Last but not least …

M I was over the moon.

N It gets on your nerves.

O Every so often, …

P He was a pain in the neck.

Q Sorry, that's out of the question.

R He went through the roof!

S No, you've got the wrong end of the stick.

T That's OTT (over the top).

U That's up to you.

V That's all very well but …

W It's out of this world.

X I agree with you to some extent.

Y Not in a million years!

Z It's a zoo out there!

2 **Match each picture to an idiom.**

3 **You're going to hear conversations that include the idioms in Exercise 1. Listen and answer the questions.**

06

- **a** Can you understand any of the idioms from the context?
- **b** Are any the same or similar in your language?

a

b

c

d

Speaking

4 **Work in pairs. Explain these idioms in your own words.**

- **a** It's as easy as ABC.
  It's very, very easy.
- **b** It went from bad to worse.
- **c** It was a piece of cake.
- **d** You've really put your foot in it.
- **e** It's anybody's guess.
- **f** I haven't got the faintest idea!
- **g** I was over the moon.
- **h** It gets on your nerves.
- **i** He was a pain in the neck.

5 **Match the idioms to the explanations.**

1. What on earth …?
2. On the one hand … on the other hand …
3. It's a good job that …
4. Last but not least …
5. Every so often, …
6. That's out of the question.
7. No, you've got the wrong end of the stick.
8. That's OTT (over the top).
9. That's all very well but …

- **a** Sometimes.
- **b** That's completely impossible.
- **c** That's fine. However, …
- **d** That's much more than is necessary.
- **e** *This introduces a question when you're extremely surprised or annoyed about something.*
- **f** *This means 'it's fortunate that'.*
- **g** *Use this to compare two different points of view.*
- **h** You have not understood the situation correctly.
- **i** *You say this to introduce the final item in a list and to say that it's just as important as the other items.*

6 **Listen again. Work in pairs. Choose six idioms you like and write six short conversations to include them. Then practise your conversations and act them out in front of the class.**

1.7 Improve your writing

In this lesson you will...

- write a letter to an exchange school.

Your school is planning to set up an exchange with a school in another country. The exchange school wants to know about languages at your school. Your teacher has asked you to write a letter about your experience of learning a language to send to the exchange school.

1 **Work in pairs. Read the letter on the opposite page. Match each paragraph of the letter to the questions below.**

   a Why do you think it's good to learn languages?
   b How will you end your letter?
   c Which languages do students learn at your school? Which languages do you learn at school? Do you speak any other languages? ***Paragraph 1***
   d When did you start learning another language? What helps you to learn?
   e What do you particularly enjoy about learning another language?
   f What are the other advantages of learning languages?

2 **With your partner, discuss how you will answer the questions in Exercise 1.**

3 **Using your answers and following the model letter on the opposite page, write a draft of your own letter.**

4 **Check your letter.**

   - Have you spelled the names of the languages correctly?
   - Have you used *-ing* forms as subjects and objects correctly? ***Learning** languages is important.* *I've always enjoyed **learning** English.*
   - Have you given examples to support your opinions?
   - Have you started and finished your letter correctly?

5 **Write the final version of your letter.**

Paragraph 1

Paragraph 2

Paragraph 3

Paragraph 4

Paragraph 5

Paragraph 6

Dear Head of Languages

At our school, we all learn English. Students can also choose to study Arabic, German or French. I'm learning English, and I've just started learning Arabic. I also know a few words of German and French.

I've always enjoyed learning English. I started when I was 6 years old. I can now watch films and TV programmes in English. The subtitles help a lot, particularly with pronunciation. I also learn a lot of new words that way.

Learning languages is important, especially when you meet someone from another country. Speaking to someone in their own language, even if it is only for a short time, makes that person feel more at ease. It makes all the difference even if you can only say 'hello', 'please' and 'thank you'.

When you learn another language, you also learn about the culture of the people who speak it, and that's really interesting. You learn that certain expressions go with certain gestures, for example, which are different from the gestures you use when speaking your own language.

I like learning phrases like 'you've got the wrong end of the stick'. When I first heard it, I didn't know what it meant! Being able to use expressions like that is really nice because it makes you feel more confident when you speak.

I'm looking forward to communicating in English with students from your school.

Yours sincerely

(your name)

1.8 Project challenge

Project 1: A guide to non-verbal communication

You're going to write a guide to non-verbal communication in your country for visitors of your own age.

1 Work in groups. Discuss what you will include in each of the following sections:

Gestures
Which gestures do people use most often and what do they mean?

Do young people and older people use different gestures?

Are there any gestures that might cause confusion?

Silence
When is silence appropriate and not appropriate?

Touch
What are the rules about touch?

Eye contact
What are the rules about eye contact?

2 Remember you can use abstract nouns, such as *friendliness*, *embarrassment* and *impatience*.

3 Can you use any of the following words and phrases?

definitely	**it makes all the difference**	**more likely to be**
even if	**a little bit**	**for example**
it's really useful	**of course**	

4 Decide how you're going to present your guide.
Are you going to:

- give a slide presentation?
- make a poster?
- produce a leaflet?
- write a magazine article?

Give reasons for your choice.

5 Write a draft of your guide.

6 Check what you have written for spelling, punctuation and grammar.

7 Write a final version.

- Was it helpful to organise your ideas in four sections: gestures, silence, touch and eye contact?
- Did you include abstract nouns and some short phrases, such as *of course, for example, even if*?

Project 2: Learn a new language!

Find out about a language you don't know and teach 10 to 15 words and simple phrases from it to your classmates.

1 Work in groups. Decide on a language and give your reasons.

2 Choose the words and phrases you want to teach. How will you choose them?

Here are some in Swedish:

Swedish	pronunciation	meaning
hej	'hay'	hello
hej då	'hay door'	goodbye
tack	'tack'	thank you
ja	'yah'	yes
nej	'nay'	no
snälla	'snella'	please
bra	'bra'	good, fine
Hur är det?	'hur air de'	How are you?
Vad heter du?	'va hiete du'	What's your name?
Var bor du?	'var bor du'	Where do you live?
Jag bor i …	'ya bor ee …'	I live in …
Välkommen!	'vel-kommen'	Welcome!
Pratar du engelska?	'prahtah du engleskah'	Do you speak English?

3 Make sure you know how to pronounce the words. You can use language websites on the internet to help you.

4 Decide how you will teach the words to your classmates.

- Will you write them on the board or will you just say them and get your classmates to repeat them?
- How will you explain their meaning? Will you use actions and gestures to explain them or will you translate them?
- Will you ask your classmates to write them down?
- Will you ask them to create dialogues and act them out?

5 Teach the class your words and phrases. Then ask them to complete the checklist to evaluate your lesson.

- Was it easy to teach and learn the words and phrases from a language you didn't know?
- Did using the words to make short dialogues help you to remember them?

1.9 Poetry

Haiku is a form of poetry that became popular in Japan in the 17th century, particularly through the work of Matsuo Bashō (1644–1694). In Japanese, haiku poems traditionally appear in a single vertical line. You say them in one breath. Why? Because a haiku aims to capture a moment in time, and a moment is short.

There are usually one or two images in a haiku, especially images from nature, and there is often a reference to a season. (Japan has four seasons: spring, summer, autumn and winter.)

07

1 In English, a haiku is often translated into a three-line poem. Read and listen to this translation of a well-known haiku. Why do you think haiku poems are popular?

Old pond
leap-splash –
a frog.
Matsuo Bashō

leap: jump from one place to another, or high in the air

splash: the sound of something hitting a liquid (like water)

08

2 Read and listen to some more haiku poems by Matsuo Bashō translated into English. First, match each one to a picture. Then answer the questions.

1
Friends part
for ever – wild geese
lost in cloud.

2
Wake, butterfly –
it's late, we've miles
to go together.

3
Violets –
how precious on
a mountain path.

a

b

c

a Which poem is about the beauty of the natural world?

b Which poem expresses sadness?

c Which poem expresses impatience?

3 Work in pairs. Talk about each of the poems in Exercise 2.

Student A: I like the first poem.

Student B: So do I. Why do you think the poet wrote it?

Student A: Perhaps he saw some geese in the sky and this made him think of friends and friendship.

Student B: What do you mean?

Student A: Well, seeing things in nature can sometimes make you think of other things. Perhaps he enjoys being with his friends and he is sad that they are all going away.

> Poets have translated haiku from Japanese into several languages, including Arabic, Gujarati, French, Spanish, Portuguese, Italian and English. They have also written original haiku in their own languages.

09

4 These two haiku poems were written in English. First, read and listen to them. Then work in pairs to answer the questions about the poems.

Grey as steel, the sea
Shimmers in the fading light:
Day slides into night.
John Foster

Shimmering heat-waves –
A hot pebble in the hand,
Light-dance on the sea.
Wendy Cope

a The title of one of these poems is 'Summer haiku'. Which one – the poem by John Foster, or the poem by Wendy Cope?

b What time of day is it in each poem?

c Which words describe movement?

d How would you describe the difference between these poems?

> **steel:** a strong metal made from iron and carbon
> **shimmers:** shines with a soft light that looks as if it is shaking
> **pebble:** a small stone

5 Describe or find a picture to illustrate each of the poems in Exercise 4.

6 Choose one of the pictures below. Write a haiku about it.

- First, work in pairs. Choose a picture and say why you have chosen it.
  I like this picture because it makes me think of …
- Working individually, read the haiku poems on pages 28 and 29 again, to give you ideas.
- Decide which of the following you are going to focus on: the season of the year, movement, smell, touch, light, sadness, happiness ...
- Write a three-line haiku.
- Read it to your partner and ask for comments.
- 10 Listen to a haiku a student wrote about the first picture.
  What do you think of it?

7 Find your own picture and use it to write a haiku. Follow the steps in Exercise 6.

Check your progress

General knowledge quiz

How much do you remember about what you've learned?

1 Which is the odd one out, and why?

French Japanese Canadian Spanish

2 If someone is bilingual, what does it mean?

3 Match the labels to the numbers on the map.

- Australia
- Indonesia
- Papua New Guinea
- Indian Ocean
- South Pacific Ocean

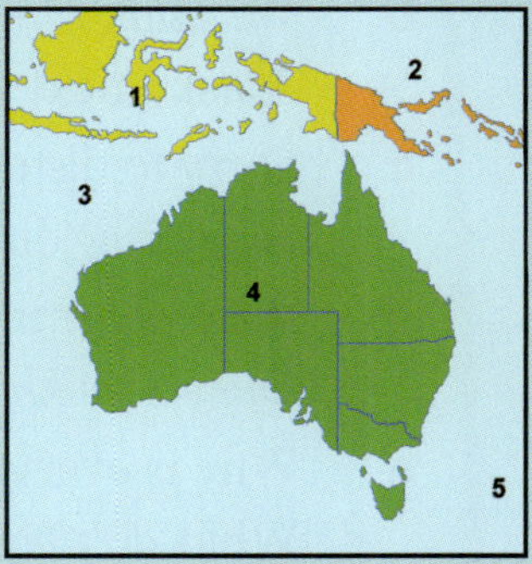

4 What is the capital of Papua New Guinea?

5 What is Tok Pisin?

6 What is this kind of symbol called and what does this one mean?

7 What does it mean in Russia if you tap the side of your head with your finger?

8 If you arrive at 11.30 'on the dot', what does this mean?

9 How do you feel if you are 'over the moon'?

10 If something is 'a piece of cake', is it easy, difficult, very big or very small?

Vocabulary

1 **Find the word for six languages in the circles.**

a n a s t C e n e o

Cantonese

b b i c A a r

c d i n i H

d h a p S i n s

e a d r i n a M n

2 **Complete the sentences with an appropriate word.**

A I sp***eak*** French to my mum and Arabic to my dad.

B Oh, so you're b...... .

A Yes, that's right. What about you?

B Well, my first l...... is Urdu but I also speak English.

A You speak English really well. I'd say you're fl...... in English.

B We use English a lot at home and I watch films in English.

A So do I, sometimes with sub......, so that I can read what the actors are saying.

3 **Choose the correct word for each idiom.**

a 'How was the maths test?'
'It was a *lot / bit / piece* of cake.'

b 'Did you watch that film right to end?'
'Oh, it was awful! It went from *good / bad / wrong* to worse.'

c 'I can't stand that kind of music.'
'I know, it really gets on your *head / mind / nerves*.'

d 'They've closed the roads near our school because they're doing a lot of building work.'
'Does it take you longer to get to school then?'
'Yes, it takes an hour. It's a pain in the *foot / neck / head*.'

Use of English

1 Here are the answers to some questions. What were the questions?

a What ***did they have for lunch?***
They had pasta for lunch.

b Which ……?
I speak Turkish and German.

c Whose ……?
It's my book.

d How many ……?
She speaks three: Hindi, English and Urdu.

e Who ……?
Aziz won the science prize.

2 Complete the sentences with an appropriate verb in the *-ing* form.

a I don't like ***being*** late for school.

b …….. too many sweets is bad for you.

c …….. football on TV is OK, but I prefer …….. to a match.

d I can spend hours …….. the guitar.

e I enjoy …….. friends at the weekend.

3 Choose the correct option in each sentence: present simple or present continuous.

a I ***don't understand*** */ 'm not understanding* what you're saying.

b We *think of / 're thinking of* going to Alaska next year.

c Sorry to disturb you. *Do you have / Are you having* dinner at the moment?

d We're learning a bit of Swedish. We *know / 're knowing* ten words already.

e Why is everyone over by the window? What *do they look at / are they looking at*?

f He *doesn't remember / isn't remembering* anything about the accident.

Summary checklist

I can

- [ ] ask and answer questions about learning languages.
- [ ] discuss the advantages of learning languages.
- [ ] identify the meaning of emojis and discuss the advantages and disadvantages of using them.
- [ ] understand a text about body language in different cultures.
- [ ] discuss what people need to know about body language in our culture.
- [ ] use English idioms in conversation.
- [ ] write a letter about my experience of learning languages to send to an exchange school.
- [ ] write a guide to non-verbal communication in our country.
- [ ] teach my classmates a few words and phrases of a new language.

2 Design and architecture

In this unit you will...

- **discuss** the shapes and packaging of everyday items
- **learn** words for three-dimensional shapes
- **describe** objects and **discuss** why they have become design classics
- **talk** about the design of buildings and their surroundings
- **read** an article about building houses from plastic bottles
- **ask** and **answer** questions in a quiz about famous buildings
- **write** a report on school buildings and facilities
- **create** a design for packaging
- **give** a presentation about a house made from recycled materials
- **read** extracts from a book about the history of pictures
- **write** a description of a picture.

Getting started

"Think of an object and a building that look good. What do you like about their design?"

Watch this!

2.1 Bars, boxes and bottles

In this lesson you will...

- use partitives (*a bunch of bananas, a piece of paper*)
- discuss shapes and the packaging of everyday items.

- **What are the five most common items you buy at the supermarket?**

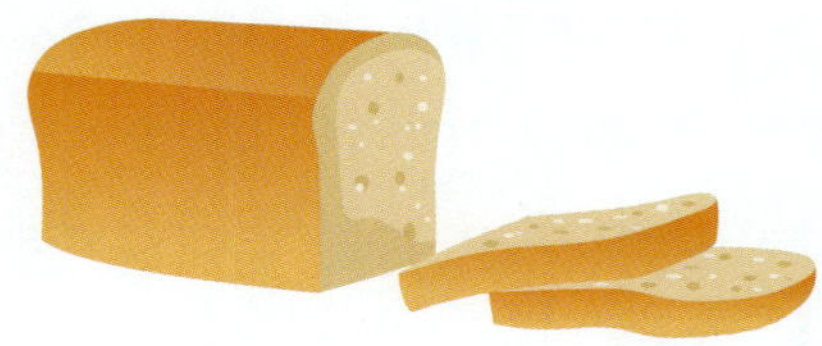

Vocabulary

1 **Work in pairs. Describe the items in the pictures using words from the list.**

~~bananas~~ biscuits orange juice bread potatoes cake soap chocolates cola toothpaste honey water tomatoes

a a bunch of ***bananas***

b a bar of ....

c a jar of ....

d a tube of ....

e a carton of ....

f a loaf of ....

g a bottle of ....

h a slice of ....

i a can of ....

j a packet of ....

k a tin of ....

l a box of ....

m a bag of ....

11 2 **Listen and check.**

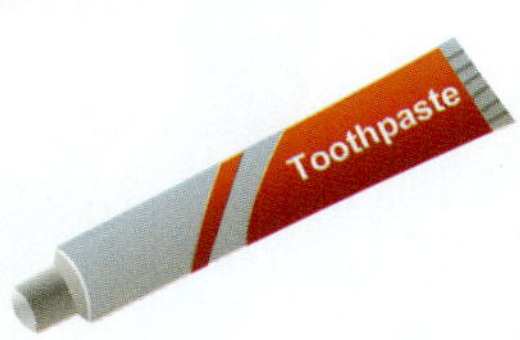

11 **3 Listen again and answer these questions.**

a What additional information is given about the following?

- the bananas
- the bread
- the cake
- the biscuits

b Which items does the woman sound surprised about, and why?

Use of English Partitives

You can use noun phrases with *of* to describe things that come in:

- containers — ***a packet of*** *biscuits*
- groups — ***a bunch of*** *bananas*
- shapes — ***a bar of*** *soap*

Partitives can be used in a lot of everyday expressions with uncountable nouns:

a piece of *advice* ***a piece of*** *paper* ***a bit of*** *information*

a bit of *salad* ***a drop of*** *water*

Language tip

Jar and *pot* are similar (*a jar of honey, a pot of mustard*). However, a jar is usually made of glass, whereas a pot can be made of metal, plastic, clay, etc.

4 Use partitive expressions to complete the shopping list.

a	*a carton of* milk	**d**	.... strawberry jam
b	.... vinegar	**e**	.... grapes
c	.... tissues	**f**	.... yoghurt

Speaking

5 Work in groups. Discuss the following:

Why do we have …

- a tube of toothpaste rather than a can of toothpaste?
- a packet of crisps rather than a jar of crisps?
- a bar of chocolate rather than a can of chocolate?
- a carton of eggs rather than a bag of eggs?

2.2 Why is an egg egg-shaped?

In this lesson you will...

- learn and use words for three-dimensional shapes
- describe imaginary situations using *if* clauses.

Key words: Maths – Geometry

cone
cube
cylinder
hemisphere
hexagonal prism
sphere
square-based pyramid
triangular prism
triangular pyramid

- **How many sides does a triangle have? What's the difference between a square and a rectangle? How many sides does a hexagon have? Is a sphere round or square?**

Vocabulary

1 **Match the words in the maths key words box to the 3D (three-dimensional) shapes.**

1 
2 
3 
4 
5 
6 
7 
8 
9 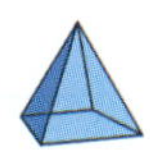

2 **A 'net' is a pattern that you can cut and fold to make a 3D shape. Match these nets to the shapes in Exercise 1.**

a 

a cube

b 

c 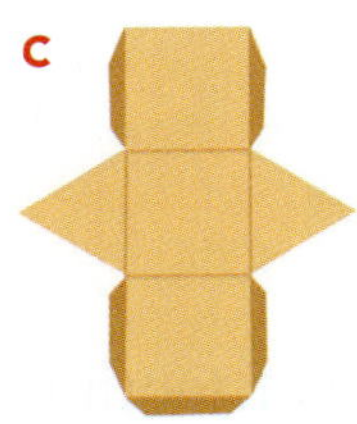

d 

Listening

12

3 **Listen to an extract from a radio programme. Who is being interviewed, and what is she talking about?**

4 **Listen again and answer the questions.**

a The author talks about two shapes. What are they?

b What examples of each does she talk about?

c What are the advantages of the shape of each object?

Reading

5 **Read the questions sent in by listeners to the radio programme. How would you answer them?**

a Why are traffic cones cone-shaped?

b Why is an egg egg-shaped?

c Is a cube the best shape for ice to keep drinks cold? Why? / Why not?

6 Read the author's answers. Compare them with what you said.

- **a** The base of a traffic cone is wider than the top, which makes it stable. If it was cylindrical, rather than conical, it would fall over easily.
- **b** Eggs are egg-shaped because if birds laid eggs that were in the shape of a sphere, they would roll out of the nest and break. If they were spherical, they would not fit together so well in the nest.
- **c** Ice cubes are served to keep drinks cold, but a spherical shape contains the same amount of frozen liquid by volume but with less surface area. This means it will melt more slowly than a cube. However, ice usually comes in cubes because they take up less space in a freezer.

7 Put the verbs in the correct form in these sentences.

- **a** If balls ***were*** (*be*) square, they ***would be*** (*be*) hard to catch.
- **b** If I .... (*have*) a spaceship, I .... (*go*) to the moon.
- **c** If everyone .... (*like*) the same kind of design and architecture, all cities .... (*look*) the same.
- **d** If we ***didn't study*** (*not study*) maths and science, we ***wouldn't be able to*** (*not be able to*) understand the world so well.
- **e** If umbrellas .... (*be*) square, they .... (*not fold up*) easily.
- **f** If your class ***entered*** (*enter*) a design competition, what ***would you make*** (*you / make*)?
- **g** If you .... (*have*) a free day tomorrow, what .... (*you / do*)?
- **h** If you .... (*be*) an architect, what kind of buildings .... (*you / choose*) to design?

Speaking

8 In pairs, ask and answer these questions.

- **a** Why is the ball used in games such as football, table tennis and golf a sphere? What would happen if it was a cube?
- **b** Why is a can of cola cylindrical? What would it be like if it was a triangular prism?
- **c** Why are bottles narrower at the top than the bottom? What would happen if it was the other way round?

Language tip

noun	adjective
cone	conical
sphere	spherical
cylinder	cylindrical

Use of English Second conditional

We can use *if* clauses to describe imaginary situations.

***If** birds **laid** eggs that were in the shape of a sphere, they **would roll** out of the nest and break.*

***If** they **were** spherical, they **would not fit** together so well in the nest.*

What do you notice about the verb tense in the *if* clause?

What do you notice about the verb form in the other clause?

Remember that you can use short forms for *would* and *would not*:

- I would – *I'd*
- they would – *they'd*
- I would not – *I wouldn't*
- They would not – *they wouldn't*

2.3 Design classics

In this lesson you will...

- describe objects and discuss why they have become design classics
- research a design classic and ask and answer questions about it.

- **A 'design classic' describes an object that is an excellent example of its kind: it doesn't go out of fashion. Can you think of any design classics?**

Listening and speaking

13

1 **Listen and match the descriptions to the objects.**

a

b

c

d

2 **Work in pairs. Describe the design classics in the pictures on page 38. Use the adjectives and expressions in the boxes to help you. Say why you think each one was successful. Listen again if you need to.**

(not) expensive
beautiful
comfortable
practical
simple
unusual

was placed sideways
to save space
is made today
modern version
originated in (country)
original version
was designed in (year)
has become popular all over the world
made in a particular shape
a thin piece of metal
variations on the original design
heart-shaped
star-shaped
square-shaped
standard symbol

3 **Find out about one of the design classics in the pictures below. Use these questions to help you.**

a When and where was it designed / produced?
b Why was it popular / successful?
c Was it expensive?
d What shape is it?
e How would you describe the design: simple, practical, beautiful?
f What is it made of?
g Is there anything unusual about it?
h Are there any variations on the original design?
i Is it still made today?

4 **Work in groups. Ask and answer the questions in Exercise 3 about the design classic you researched.**

2.4 Just the place

In this lesson you will...

- understand the detail of descriptions of three buildings
- talk about the design of buildings and their surroundings.

- **Which is the most interesting building in your town or city?**

Listening

14 **1 Work in pairs. Before you listen, look at the pictures and say where you think each building is. Then listen to the descriptions and find out if you were right.**

2 Work in pairs. Which materials were used for each of the buildings in the photos?

bamboo	concrete	clay	metal	wood
brick	earth	glass	stone	

Speaking

3 Work in groups. Describe each of the buildings in as much detail as you can. Use these words and phrases to help you.

traditional	respect for nature	penthouse apartment
log cabin	average temperature	façade
built by hand	apartment block	balcony
living room	hilly landscape	skylight windows
school buildings	towers	curved roof
brick walls	floors	

a

b

Use of English Relative clauses beginning with prepositions

Read these two sentences.

There is a living room with a large window. You can look out over a pond from the large window.

Notice how you can combine them using a relative clause beginning with a preposition.

There is a living room with a large window **from which** *you can look out over a pond.*

Now read these two sentences, and notice how you can combine them using a relative clause beginning with a preposition.

The students at this school in Thailand have their lessons in classrooms made entirely from bamboo and earth. Respect for nature is an important part of the curriculum for these students.

The students at this school in Thailand, **for whom** *respect for nature is an important part of the curriculum, have their lessons in classrooms made entirely from bamboo and earth.*

4 Combine these sentences using relative clauses. Remember to use *which* for things and *whom* for people.

a Denmark is well known for its interesting modern architecture. The Wave is a stunning example of interesting modern architecture. (use ***of***)

b There are skylight windows. Light enters every apartment through these windows. (use ***through***)

c The architects have designed important buildings in Denmark and other parts of the world. The Wave has won several awards for the architects. (use ***for***)

Language tip

Notice these compound nouns for describing buildings: *log cabin, living room, school building, brick wall, apartment block, penthouse apartment, skylight window.*

Speaking

5 Work in groups. Discuss the buildings in the pictures in this lesson.

a What do you like about them?

b What's the connection between each building and its environment?

c

2.5 Homes in the desert

In this lesson you will...

- read an article about building houses from plastic bottles
- discuss the project described in the article.

- **Which are the hottest places on Earth? Which are the coldest places?**

Reading

1 **Look at the article below. Focus on the title and the photo. What do you think the article is about?**

15 2 **Read and listen to the article. Why do you think the journalist chose to write about Tateh Lehbib?**

Meet the refugee building homes in the desert from plastic bottles

Engineer Tateh Lehbib has designed houses for refugee camps that are resistant to desert heat, sandstorms and torrential rain

'I was born in a sun-dried brick house,' says Tateh Lehbib. 'The roof was made of sheets of zinc – one of the best heat conductors. My family and I had to endure high temperatures, rain and sandstorms that would sometimes take the roof off.'

Tateh, 27, studied renewable energy at Tlemcen University in Algeria, from where he went on to study energy efficiency at Las Palmas University, Gran Canaria, Spain.

'When I came back to the camp, I decided to build a place for my grandmother to live that was more comfortable and more worthy of her.'

All he needed was 6000 empty plastic bottles.

* * *

Vocabulary

3 How many words for building materials can you find in the article?

4 In pairs, find these words in the text and try to work out their meaning.

- a sun-dried
- b endure
- c layers
- d belongings
- e spacious

5 Work in groups. Discuss these questions. You can use the words in the environmental science key words box to help you.

- a What were the problems with the house in which Tateh grew up?
- b How do you think Tateh's studies helped him in his project to build houses in the desert?
- c What are the advantages of the materials Tateh uses for his buildings?
- d What are the advantages of the design?
- e Are there any disadvantages of the design?
- f How has Tateh's building project helped the local community?

6 In your groups, draw and label a diagram of one of Tateh's houses to explain how it's built and how it works.

Key words: Environmental science

air flow
energy efficiency
heat conductor
heat flow
resistant (to heat)

The bottles are filled with sand and straw. Then they are placed next to each other in a circle. More layers of bottles are added, making a circular wall. Once the main structure is created, the walls are covered with cement and limestone, and then painted white to reflect the sun's rays and to keep the room temperature cool.

'This prevents the house from getting hot, even lowering the temperature to 5 °C,' said Tateh.

He decided that the roof should have two layers to improve air flow and to make it more resistant to heat. The first covering consists of mats made from recycled plastic and the second is a layer of cement.

The round shape of the building was carefully chosen as well. According to Tateh, the shape prevents 'light rays entering directly, which reduces heat flow'. It also prevents sand from accumulating on the outside of the structure during sandstorms.

Tateh's constructions were not always welcomed by the refugees, for whom a good strong house could not possibly be built with plastic bottles.

'At first, they called me "the crazy bottle man". Once they had seen the houses with their own eyes, people understood the project better,' he said.

Tateh realises that it's hard to fit furniture and carpets in a round house.

'We are testing alternatives so that the house is round outside but square inside, to make it possible for people to put their belongings on shelves,' he said. 'It is also important to make the house bigger, more spacious, because the Sahrawis need a very wide room to welcome guests and make tea.'

'These homes also help create jobs in a place where there are hardly any. It takes four people to pick up the bottles, four others to fill them, and four builders to construct the house. Drivers are also required to transport sand and bottles,' Tateh said. 'In fact, we are creating an industry around plastic houses,' he added.

2.6 Famous buildings

In this lesson you will...

- ask and answer questions in a quiz about famous buildings
- use questions beginning with prepositions.

- **How many famous buildings can you think of? Do they have anything in common?**

Speaking

1 **Work with a partner. Take turns to ask and answer the questions in the quiz on the opposite page.**

Listening

16

2 **Listen and check your answers.**

3 **Listen again. Write down one more piece of information about each place.**

4 **Compare your answers to Exercise 3 with your partner's answers. Did you write down the same piece of information?**

Use of English Questions beginning with prepositions

It's sometimes clearer to put the preposition at the beginning of a question.

***In** which country is the ancient city of Petra?*
sounds better than:
*Which country is the ancient city of Petra **in**?*

***From** which building can you watch the sun set twice in less than a minute?*
sounds better than:
*Which building can you watch the sun set twice in less than a minute **from**?*

5 **Rewrite the following questions, putting the preposition first. Then ask and answer them with a partner.**

a Which city is the Empire State Building in?
b Which country did Marco Polo set sail from on his travels to Asia?
c Which Spanish island is Mount Teide on?
d Which country did the Portuguese explorer, Vasco da Gama, sail to in 1498?
e Who did the French give the Statue of Liberty to in 1886?

6 **Work in pairs. Write two multiple-choice questions to add to the quiz. Then ask and answer your questions around the class.**

1 In which ancient ruined city are you standing if you can see the Andes mountains?

- a Ur, in Iraq
- b Machu Picchu, in Peru
- c Petra, in Jordan

2 From which building can you see the Eiffel Tower?

- a the Colosseum, in Rome
- b the Kremlin, in Moscow
- c the Louvre Museum, in Paris

3 For whom was the Taj Mahal built? It was built ...

- a for Shah Jahan, in memory of his wife.
- b for Shah Jahan, to celebrate his wedding.
- c for Genghis Khan, as a palace.

4 In which country is the ancient city of Petra?

a Italy b Jordan c Malaysia

5 In which city is al-Masjid al-Haram, the biggest mosque in the world?

a Istanbul b Mecca c Cairo

6 For which event was the Beijing National Stadium built?

- a the 2010 World Cup
- b the 2009 Asian Games
- c the 2008 Olympic Games

7 From which building can you watch the sun set twice in less than a minute?

- a the Eiffel Tower in Paris
- b the Burj Khalifa building in Dubai
- c the CN Tower in Toronto, Canada

8 On which building does the sun cast a shadow like a snake at the spring equinox?

- a the Great Pyramid at Giza, in Egypt
- b the Pyramid of El Castillo at Chichén Itzá in Mexico
- c the temple of Angkor Wat in Cambodia

9 On which building is there a roof designed to look like the sails on a ship?

- a the Sydney Opera House in Sydney, Australia
- b the Parthenon in Athens, Greece
- c the Sagrada Familia cathedral in Barcelona, Spain

10 To which city do you go if you want to see the Alhambra Palace?

- a Granada, in the south of Spain
- b Marrakech, in Morocco
- c Ankara, in Turkey

2.7 Improve your writing

In this lesson you will...

- write a report on school buildings and facilities.

Your headteacher wants to know what improvements students would like to see to the buildings and facilities at your school.

1 Work in groups. Talk about improvements you would like to see. Note down your ideas.

What do you think should be done?

We should consider having …

To me the most important thing would be to …

I think it would also be good to …

I think that's a good idea.

We could suggest having …

I'd like a locker in which I could store my books and personal belongings.

If we had solar panels, we would have more energy-efficient buildings.

If we had a basketball court and a football pitch, we could do more outdoor sports.

2 Your English teacher has asked you to present your ideas in the form of a report. Look at the example on the opposite page and the English teacher's comments. Match each comment a–j to a number 1–10.

3 Write a report giving your group's ideas and suggestions. Follow these steps.

Step 1: Write a draft. Organise your ideas into paragraphs:

- Paragraph 1: the buildings
- Paragraph 2: outdoor areas
- Paragraph 3: facilities
- Paragraph 4: other ideas

Step 2: Check your draft.

- Have you included expressions such as *Firstly, …, Secondly, …, Finally, …, With regard to, For example, also*?
- Have you checked the grammar and the spelling?

Step 3: Write the final version.

A report on school buildings and facilities

There are several things that we think can be improved. [1] Some of the school buildings are old-fashioned and badly designed. [2] For example, one wall of the science block consists mostly of windows, which means it's very hot in summer and very cold in winter, especially on the upper floors. It [3] also means you have to have the blinds down most of the time in summer because it's too bright. [4] Some of the rooms in the basement have very little natural light, so you have to have the lights on most of the time.

[5] We think that the outdoor areas could be improved. At break time and lunchtime we don't only need somewhere to play football and other sports, we also need places in the shade where we can sit and have some quiet time, preferably with a few benches.

[6] With regard to [7] facilities, we would really welcome having a small café. School is from 8.30 until 3.00 with only two short breaks, so if we had a café we'd be able to buy a drink and a sandwich or some fruit. We wouldn't get hungry, thirsty and tired. We would also like onsite recycling bins [8] in which we could put plastic and paper.

[9] We would like to have a drama studio. A lot of students are interested in doing drama and at the moment we only have the main hall, which is often used for other purposes.

We appreciate [10] to have the chance to give our ideas and we hope that our suggestions are helpful.

Teacher's comments

- **a** 'With regard to' is a good way to introduce the topic of the paragraph. *7*
- **b** Add 'Finally' here to show that this is the last point. 'Finally, we would like to …'
- **c** Add 'Secondly' here. 'Secondly, we think the outdoor areas …'
- **d** Grammar mistake. This should be 'We appreciate having …'.
- **e** It would be a good idea to use 'signpost' expressions like 'Firstly', 'Secondly', 'Finally' to show the reader where a new point begins. 'Firstly, some of the school buildings …' *1*
- **f** Start a new paragraph here because you're moving on to a new point, about facilities.
- **g** This a good use of 'also' to make an additional point.
- **h** This is a good use of a relative clause beginning with a preposition.
- **i** This is good. It's important to give examples of what you mean.
- **j** You could start this sentence with 'By contrast', to show that you are going to make a contrasting point. 'By contrast, some of the rooms …'

2.8 Project challenge

Project 1: A design for packaging

You're going to design the packaging for a product of your choice.

1 Work in groups. Decide what kind of product you're going to choose.

- chocolates (or a bar of chocolate)
- biscuits
- soap
- shampoo
- an energy bar
- a fruit drink

2 Decide on the packaging.

What's the best shape?

What material should we use?

What colour should it be?

What size should it be?

3 Draw a sketch of your product and the packaging. Label the sketch.

4 Discuss any improvements you could make.

5 Draw the final version of your packaging. If possible, make a model to show the class.

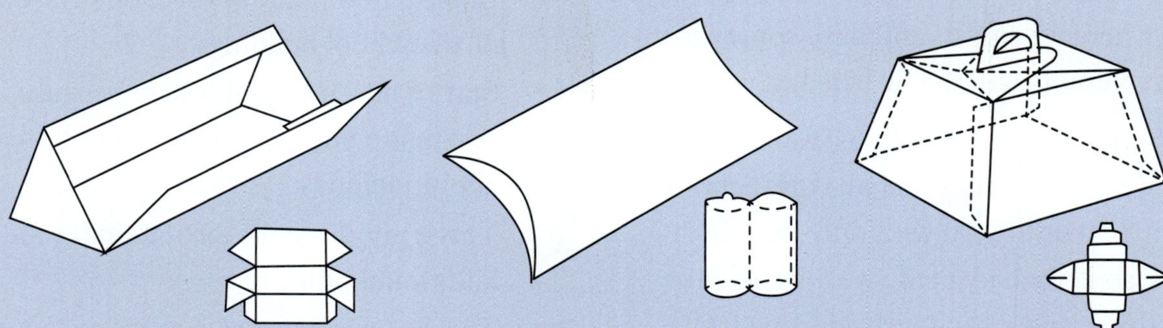

6 Present your packaging to the class. Give reasons for your choice of shape, colour and material.

7 Ask the class for their comments.

- How did working in groups, rather than on your own, help?
- When the class gave their comments, which comments did you agree with? Which comments did you not agree with?

Project 2: A presentation

You are going to create a presentation about a house made from recycled materials.

1 Work in groups. Research houses built from recycled materials. Choose the one you like best and answer these questions.

a Where is it?

b What is it made from?

c Where did the materials come from and why do you think they were chosen?

d What is special about it?

e What are the advantages and disadvantages of the building?

2 Use your answers to the questions above to write a three-minute presentation.

- Find pictures to illustrate the information.
- Each student in your group can present one aspect of the information you have found.

3 Use this outline to structure your presentation:

- Introduce the subject of the talk.
  We're going to tell you about …
- Tell your audience what you're going to talk about.
  We're going to start by talking about …
  Then we're going to …
  Finally, …
- Present the building you've chosen.
  So, first of all, the building we've chosen is in …
- Close the presentation and invite questions.
  Thank you very much for listening.
  Now, have you got any questions?

4 Give the presentation.

5 Ask the class for their comments.

A house made from old shipping containers

- What did you learn from doing the research for this project?
- When the class gave their comments, which comments did you agree with? Which comments did you not agree with?

2.9 Non-fiction

17 **1 Read about and listen to *A History of Pictures for Children* and about David Hockney. Why do you think he and Martin Gayford wrote the book?**

A History of Pictures for Children is a book written by David Hockney and Martin Gayford. It takes the reader on a journey from early cave paintings to the pictures we can make on our digital devices.

18 **2 Read and listen to the text on the next two pages. Answer these questions.**

- a What impresses David Hockney about the way Chinese artists work?
- b Does he only talk about painters in the past, or does he talk about painters today?
- c What connection does he see between Chinese painting and writing?
- d What does he like about the picture?

3 Find examples of the following in what David Hockney writes.

- a He asks the reader (or himself) a question.
- b He uses the first person, 'I'.
- c He writes as if he's speaking to you.
- d He gives examples to illustrate his ideas.
- e He uses adjectives and adverbs to give a clear impression of what he's describing.

4 Choose a picture that you could include in a history of pictures for children. Write a description of it, answering these questions.

- Why do you like it?
- What's interesting about the technique?

5 Values The French painter Edgar Degas said, 'Art is not what you see, but what you make others see.' What do you think he meant?

DAVID: What makes a mark interesting? I think it's movement – the way an artist uses the pencil or brush. You can often see whether they have made the line very fast or quite slowly.

Chinese painters used to practise by drawing the same images over and over again. Let's say they were drawing a bird. They might start with ten marks, then slowly get it down to three or four. I once watched a young Chinese artist painting cats, placing every mark perfectly. The characters of Chinese writing are closely linked with painting, too. Tiny changes in the marks create entirely new meanings.

WU ZHEN Leaf from an album of bamboo drawings, 1350

30

MUQI *Six Persimmons*, 13th century

In the 13th century the Chinese priest and painter Muqi created this delicate picture of six pieces of fruit with ink on silk. He hardly made any marks at all – you can almost count the number of brushstrokes. Yet he still managed to make each piece of fruit look different.

At this time Chinese artists didn't often use colour, so the way they used ink and controlled the brush was especially important. One writer on art in the Ming dynasty counted twenty-six different ways to paint rocks and twenty-seven ways to paint leaves on trees!

31

Check your progress

General knowledge quiz

How much can you remember about what you've learned?

1 What are these three-dimensional shapes called?

2 Why are eggs egg-shaped? Give two reasons.

3 What is this kind of lamp called?

4 It's a thin piece of metal that is made in a particular shape. It appeared in the 1890s and became the most popular way of keeping sheets of paper together. What is it?

5 What do you call a traditional house, usually found in rural areas of the United States, made of pieces of wood taken from the forest?

6 Why is zinc not a good material for the roof of a house in a hot country?

7 It's an ancient city in Jordan. Its buildings are half cut out of rock and half built. It is known as the 'Rose City', because of the colour of the rock. Its name begins with P. What is it called?

8 In which country is Machu Picchu?

9 In which city is the Louvre Museum?

10 Where is the Burj Khalifa building?

Vocabulary

1 **Complete these words for three-dimensional shapes.**

a c o *n e*
b s p h _ _ _
c c y l i n _ _ _
d p y r a _ _ _

2 **What are these materials?**

a You can see through it and you use it in windows.
b You can make furniture from it. It's a hard material that comes from trees.
c Copper, iron and zinc are examples of this material.
d This is made by mixing cement with sand and water.
e It's a light building material that comes from a tall, thin plant. It's from the grass family but it's very strong.

3 **Match the words to the definitions.**

penthouse skylight balcony tower façade

a The whole of the front of a building.
b A small window set into the roof.
c A small area attached to the outside wall of a building, where you can stand or sit.
d An expensive apartment on the top floor of a building.
e A tall narrow building or part of a building.

Use of English

1 Use the prompts to write sentences to describe imaginary situations.

a If you .... (*find*) a gold ring in the street, what .... (*you / do*)?

If you found a gold ring in the street, what would you do?

b If you .... (*can*) travel anywhere, where .... (*you / go*)?

c If you .... (*can*) change one thing about your school, what .... (*it / be*)?

d If I .... (*get*) 100% in a maths exam, I .... (*be*) very pleased.

e If a friend .... (*tell*) me a secret, I .... (*not / tell*) anyone.

2 Make two sentences into one.

a The Colosseum is one of Rome's most famous buildings. Gladiators fought to the death in this place. (use ***in which***)

The Colosseum, in which gladiators fought to the death, is one of Rome's most famous buildings.

b My great-grandparents now live in an apartment in the city centre. This house was built for them. (use ***for whom***)

c The results of the design competition will be announced next month. We have made a jewellery box for the competition. (use ***for which***)

d *Sherlock Holmes* was a great success for the author. The new TV series is based on it. (use ***on which***)

3 Use the prompts to write questions for these answers. Start each one with a preposition.

a Q: city / the White House / ?

In which city is the White House?

A: It's in Washington DC.

b Q: island / Mount Fuji / ?

A: It's on Honshu Island.

c Q: river / Tower Bridge / ?

A: It's over the Thames in London.

d Q: city / the volcano Popocatépetl / ?

A: You can see it from Mexico City.

e Q: ocean / the Amazon river / ?

A: It flows into the Atlantic.

Summary checklist

I can

- [ ] discuss the shapes and packaging of everyday objects.
- [ ] identify three-dimensional shapes.
- [ ] explain why certain shapes are suited to certain objects.
- [ ] talk about why certain items have become design classics.
- [ ] describe the features of buildings and what they are made of.
- [ ] talk about the connections between buildings and their environment.
- [ ] write a report suggesting improvements to school buildings and facilities.
- [ ] design packaging for a product and give a presentation about a house.

3 Our society

In this unit you will...

- **listen to** people's opinions about their city
- **read** an article about a project to improve a neighbourhood
- **consider** the advantages and disadvantages of living in the country or a city
- **discuss** ways you can make a difference in your community
- **read** and **understand** an article about the happiest nation in the world
- **find out** about a school where lessons to promote happiness are part of the school day
- **write** a letter to the town council
- **design** a mural
- **organise** an event to raise money for a school trip
- **read** poems written by school students
- **write** a poem about childhood memories.

Getting started

"A 'society' is a group of people who live together and share customs and laws. An 'individual' is a person who is not part of a group. Is it important to be both an 'individual' and a 'member of society'? Why/Why not?"

Watch this!

3.1 My city

In this lesson you will...

- listen to people's opinions about their city
- use clauses ending in prepositions.

- **How many adjectives can you think of to describe your town or city?**

Listening

19 **1** **Listen to people describing their cities. Do they like where they live?**

2 **Listen again. Which adjectives do the people use to describe their cities? Make a list.**

attractive, ...

20 **3** **You're now going to hear Timor and Shasha talking about the cities they live in. What are the main differences between them?**

4 **Which phrases and sentences are used to describe photo 1? Which are used to describe photo 2?**

a lively neighbourhood	a shopping centre	an apartment block
car-free	green spaces	narrow streets
overlooking the water	traffic congestion	raised walkways

Photo 1

Use of English Prepositions at the end of a clause

In spoken English, it sounds very formal if you say, 'There are benches on which you can sit.' It's more common to put the preposition (in this case, *on*) at the end of the clause:

There are benches (that) you can sit **on**.

You could also say:

There are benches ***to sit on***.

Again, the preposition *on* comes at the end. Timor uses this structure when he says:

There are restaurants with a wide range of food ***to choose from***.

5 Complete the sentences with the correct preposition. Then listen to Timor and Shasha's descriptions of their cities again to check your answers.

- a There was always someone I could play ....
- b There are also plenty of things for people to complain ....
- c There aren't enough parks and places to relax ....
- d That's something you've probably never heard .... !
- e There's always someone she can talk ....

Speaking

6 Work in pairs. Use the phrases in Exercise 4 and the sentences in Exercise 5 to reconstruct what Timor and Shasha said about their cities.

7 Work in small groups. Discuss your own town or city. Talk about what's good about it and what could be improved.

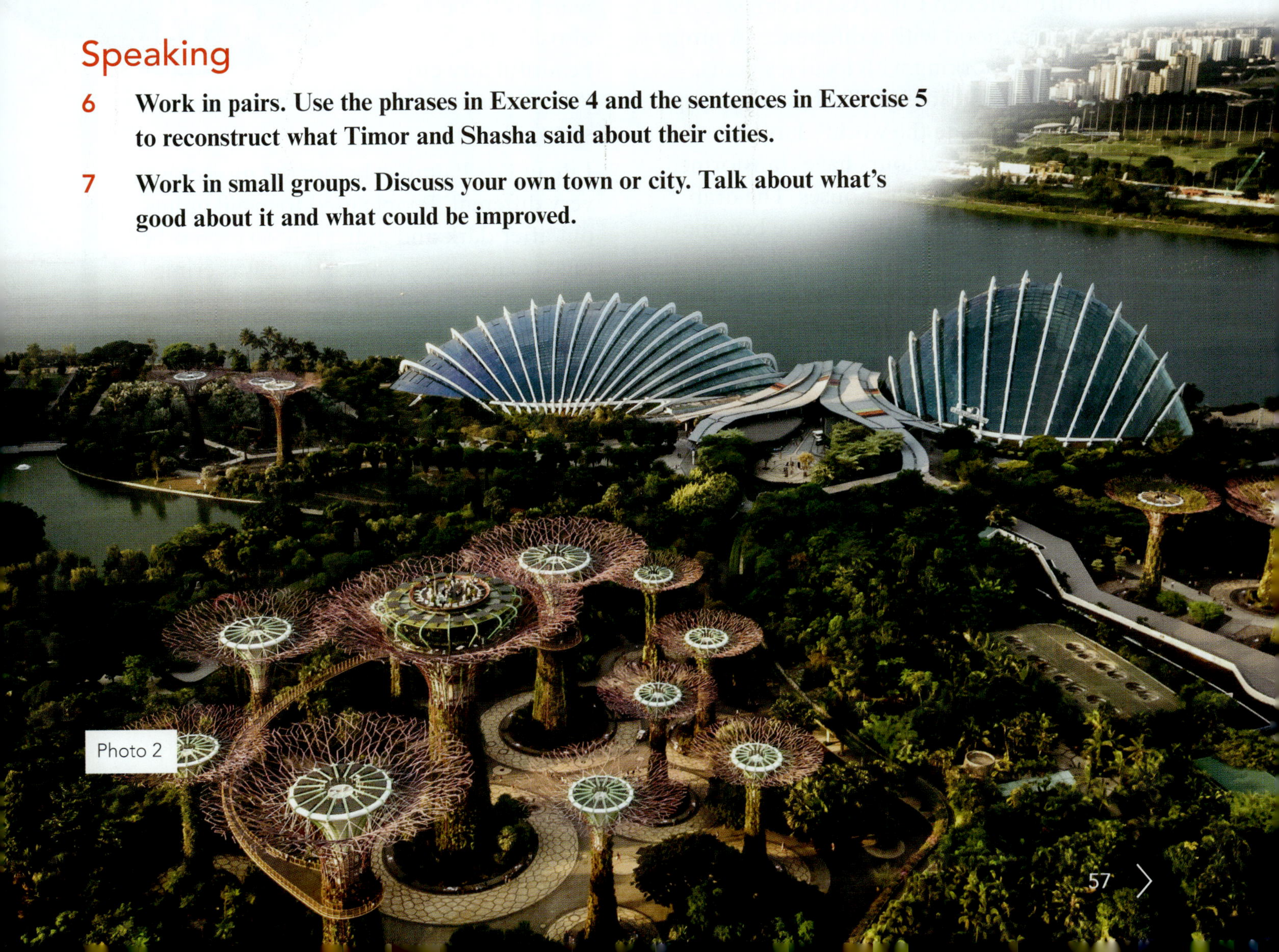

Photo 2

3.2 A neighbourhood with a difference

In this lesson you will...

- read an article about a project to improve a neighbourhood
- discuss ways in which a neighbourhood can be improved.

- **What makes an ideal neighbourhood?**

Reading

1 **Look at the photo and read the text. What is unusual about this neighbourhood?**

This is Las Palmitas, a neighbourhood that overlooks the city of Pachuca, 90 kilometres north of Mexico City. As you can see, it's a neighbourhood with a difference. A group of artists, working with local residents, painted the façades of 209 houses in bright colours to create the world's largest mural of its kind. The colours have transformed the appearance of the houses. The drab, grey, cement-covered walls have become a rainbow of colours.

'It has been a community effort, as each household has participated in some way,' said project director Enrique Gomez. The aim of the project was to make people feel better about where they lived and to bring them together.

'The neighbourhood changed completely. The colours gave it life,' says Doña Chela, a local resident.

First, all the houses were painted white, to symbolise that all the residents were equal. Then the artists worked with the residents to paint the houses in a variety of colours. Bright swirls of colour sweep across several houses to form a pattern that illustrates the city's nickname, which is 'la bella airosa' – the beautiful airy city ('airy' because the wind is often quite strong there).

Life in Las Palmitas before the project was very different. People used to avoid going out after dark and didn't talk to each other much. There were gangs, there was crime and there were social problems. Enrique Gomez was himself a gang member before he became a muralist. He managed to win the trust of young people in the neighbourhood and to persuade local residents to work together on the mural. This reduced violence in the area and helped to develop community spirit.

'It's very satisfying,' said Alfonso Reyes, a local resident. 'In the morning you wake up and look around and see the colours that surround you. It's very pretty. You go out and say, "Ah, everything is so nicely painted and fixed up."'

Vocabulary

2 Find these words in the text and choose the correct meaning.

1	drab	a	not colourful	b	rough
2	has participated	a	has given money	b	has taken part
3	swirls	a	curved shapes	b	squares
4	nickname	a	informal name	b	proper name
5	reduced	a	increased	b	decreased

Key words: Social studies

community spirit
crime
gang (member)
neighbourhood
social problems
violence

3 Find a word in the text that means …

a an area of a town or city that people live in
b people who live in a particular place
c a picture that is painted on a wall
d changed completely in a way that improves something
e organised groups of people who are often involved in crime
f someone who paints large pictures on a wall
g the belief that someone is good and honest

4 Answer the questions. Try to use the words in the social studies key word box in your answers.

a What was the purpose of the project in Las Palmitas?
b Has it been successful? Give reasons to support your answer.
c How did the project encourage community spirit?
d Do you think Enrique Gomez was a good choice to lead the project? Why?
e Why do you think the artists and residents used bright colours to paint the houses instead of leaving them white?
f Is there a connection between the appearance of an area and the way people feel and behave? Why?

Speaking

5 Work in groups. Discuss this question.

What would you do to improve the quality of life in your neighbourhood?

Some of the buildings are quite drab. I'd paint them in bright colours.

I'd paint the benches in the town square.

We could get people to work together on a mural.

3.3 Town or country?

In this lesson you will...

- consider the advantages and disadvantages of living in the country or a city
- use the second conditional with *unless* and *I wish ..., if only.*

- **Look at the photo below. What do you think it would be like to live in this place?**

Reading

1 **Read the opinions. Who do you agree with? Do you prefer the country or the city?**

I live in a village in the country and I love the freedom you have here. You can go on bike rides. You can swim in the lake in summer. You can have picnics. The only problem is that there aren't many buses. So when I get older, it might be different, and perhaps I wouldn't stay here unless I had a car. But at the moment, I think if I lived in the city, I'd be like a fish out of water. *Tasha*

In the city, you can walk everywhere or you can get a bus, and all the shops and things you need are there. But I like the peace and quiet of the countryside, especially for holidays. Sometimes I wish we lived there all the time, but it wouldn't be good for my parents because their jobs are in the city. *Adil*

I'd prefer to live in the city if I had the choice. In the country there's nothing to do for people my age. It's quite boring! If only I lived in a city like Ankara or Istanbul! That would be great. *Emine*

I wish I lived in the country, so that I could ride my bike to school. I used to live in a small village and I liked it a lot better there! Now, we live in a big city. It's so busy – more traffic, more pollution and more noise! There's more crime too. *Kaher*

Would I like to live in the country if I had the chance? I'm in two minds. I would and I wouldn't. I would because it's very quiet; I wouldn't because there's nothing to do. And I wouldn't want to live in a city, unless it was somewhere like Singapore, with lots of parks and green spaces. Then I'd have the best of both worlds. *Nisha*

People say I live in the middle of nowhere. It's true! I live on a farm: it takes half an hour to get to the nearest shop and it's 15 kilometres from the nearest town. But I like living here, and I think I'll stay because I love the outdoor life and I enjoy giving my parents a hand on the farm. If only I didn't live so far from my friends. *Mansur*

2 Read the opinions again and answer the questions.

a Who prefers the city?
b Who prefers the country?
c Who can see the advantages of both?

3 Find these idioms in the text. Think of another way of saying each one.

a I'd be *like a fish out of water*.
b I'm *in two minds*.
c I'd have *the best of both worlds*.
d I live *in the middle of nowhere*.
e I enjoy *giving* my parents *a hand* on the farm.

4 Use the correct form of the verb in brackets to complete these sentences.

a If only we ***had*** (*have*) a house near the beach!
b I ...... (*ride*) my bike every day if I ...... (*live*) in the country.
c I wish I ...... (*live*) on a farm!
d I ...... (*not cycle*) to school unless there ...... (*be*) a cycle path.
e If only I ...... (*not / have to*) get up so early!
f I wish I ...... (*can*) have riding lessons.

Writing

5 Read the texts in Exercise 1 again. Which person's opinion is closest to your own? Adapt what he / she says, making any changes to express your own opinion.

Speaking

6 Work in groups. Discuss this question: Where would you like to live when you're an adult? Try to use some of the phrases in Exercise 3.

If I had the choice, I'd prefer to live in the city because there's more to do there.
If I lived in the country / city, I'd ...
I wouldn't want to live in ..., because ...
I wish I lived in ...
If only ...
I wouldn't ... unless ...

Use of English
Second conditional with *unless*, *I wish ...*, *if only*

Remember that you learned about the second conditional in Lesson 2.2.

If I had *the choice,* ***I'd prefer*** *to live in the city.*

Note that you can put the *if* clause second:

I'd prefer *to live in the city* ***if I had*** *the choice.*

You can also use *unless* instead of *if not* in second conditional sentences.

I wouldn't stay here ***unless*** *I had a car = I wouldn't stay here if I didn't have a car.*

You can use *I wish / If only* to say that you would like something to be different. *If only* is stronger than *I wish*. Each expression is followed by the past simple, even though it refers to the present.

I wish I lived *in the country, so that I could ride my bike to school.*

If only I lived *in a city like Ankara or Istanbul!*

› 3.4 You and your community

In this lesson you will...

- discuss ways you can make a difference in your community
- use the *-ing* form after verbs, adjectives and prepositions.

- **Give an example of an occasion when you have helped someone or when someone has helped you.**

Reading

1 **Read the leaflet 'Six ways to make a difference'. What kind of activities does it mention and why do these activities 'make a difference'?**

Six ways to make a difference

1 Be a volunteer

Have you considered volunteering? **Volunteers** are not paid, of course, but they do valuable work. So if you're keen on doing something to help the local community, find out about getting involved.

2 Organise a litter collection

You always put litter in a bin instead of throwing it on the ground but not everybody is like you! Could you be responsible for cleaning up your local area? **How about organising a litter collection**? By getting your friends to help you, it won't take long, and you'll enjoy doing it.

3 Give help to someone who needs it

Would you like to do something that involves **helping someone on a regular basis**, by doing their shopping for them, for example?

4 Organise an event for charity

Are you interested in organising an event for charity? Are you good at getting people to do things? Can you suggest ways of **raising money** for **good causes**? What about having a cake sale at your school?

5 Set up a community group (a sports club, a music group …)

Are you enthusiastic about playing music in a group or about playing a sport? Then perhaps you can organise an informal and friendly **community group** in your area for people who might feel a bit nervous about joining groups.

6 Help to protect the environment

Are you worried about the future of the planet? Have you thought of getting involved with a local **environmental group**? You might just start by collecting plastic bottles for recycling, or by setting up a group to cycle to school.

Speaking

2 **Work in pairs. Discuss this question:**
If you had to choose one of the suggestions in the leaflet, which would it be, and why?

3 **Work in pairs. Ask and answer these questions.**

- a Do you know anyone who is a **volunteer**? What do they do?
- b How would you **organise a litter collection**?
- c Who might need **help on a regular basis**?
- d Can you think of the name of a **charity**? What does it do?
- e How do people **raise money** for charities?
- f What other **good causes** do you know about?
- g What is a **community group**? Can you think of any?
- h Do you belong to any **clubs** at school or in your local area? What are they? Are there any you would like to belong to?
- i Are there any **environmental groups** in your local area? What do they do?

4 **The verbs, adjectives and prepositions in these sentences are all followed by the *-ing* form. Choose a suitable verb to complete them.**

- a Our teacher suggested .... a book sale to raise money. I think that's a good idea.
- b We're thinking of .... our headteacher to let us have some space for a garden.
- c I'd like to walk to school instead of .... to school by car every day.
- d I'm fed up with .... so much litter in the streets.
- e I've just finished .... a poster to encourage people to use less plastic.
- f You can save a lot of money by .... your own salad and vegetables.

Use of English
Verbs, adjectives and prepositions followed by the *-ing* form

Remember that some verbs are followed by the *-ing* form.

*Have you **considered** volunteer**ing**?*

Adjectives and prepositions are also followed by the *-ing* form.

*Are you **good at** gett**ing** people to do things?*

*You always put litter in a bin **instead of** throw**ing** it on the ground.*

How many more examples can you find in the leaflet in Exercise 1?

Listening and writing

21 5 **Listen to students talking about 'Six ways to make a difference'. Do they use the same verbs as you did in Exercise 4?**

6 **Imagine you are in the group with the students in Exercise 5. Continue the conversation about how you can make a difference.**

3.5 Focus on ... Finland

In this lesson you will...

- read and understand an article about the happiest nation in the world
- discuss what makes a country a good place to live.

- **Where is Finland? What do you know about it?**

Reading

1 **Read the article. If you had to tell someone three interesting things about Finland, what would you tell them?**

Is everybody happy?

The World Happiness Report compares countries to find out how people feel about where they live. It looks at income, freedom, trust, healthy life expectancy, social support and generosity.

According to the most recent report, Finland is the happiest nation in the world. It was top of the table, followed by Denmark, Norway and Iceland.

And you don't have to be Finnish to be happy. You just have to live there! Immigrants to Finland are also the happiest in the world. 'It's not about Finnish DNA. It's the way life is lived,' says John Helliwell, professor of Economics at the University of British Columbia.

Finns pay quite a lot of money in tax, but they have trust in their government, they are generous and they have a great sense of community. 'They do care about each other,' Professor Helliwell says. 'That's the kind of place people want to live.'

According to one of the editors of the report, people are happier if they live in societies where there aren't big differences between rich and poor, so that most people can enjoy a similar quality of life. In Finland, healthcare and education are free. Half of Finns give regularly to charity and almost a third regularly give up time to volunteer.

School students in Finland are not only happy in their daily lives, they also enjoy life at school and do well. The typical ratio of teachers to students is 1 : 12. At the age of 15, in maths and science, Finnish students are in sixth place when compared with other countries.

Children in Finland don't have to start school until they are seven. They rarely have homework until they are at secondary school. They have very few tests and exams. They have 75 minutes of free time during the school day (whereas in the USA students only have 27 minutes). And they have a summer break that lasts 10 to 11 weeks.

You can see why Finland is number 1 in the happiness league!

FACT FILE

Finland

Capital: Helsinki
Population: 5.5 million
Life expectancy: 81.73 years
Wealth: GDP USD$48,685 per capita

Speaking

Did You Know?

- Finland's nickname is 'The Land of the Midnight Sun'.
- It's famous for the spectacular Northern Lights (the *aurora borealis*).
- It's got a snow village, with an ice hotel.

2 **Work in pairs. Answer these questions, using the words in the economics key words box where possible.**

- **a** Do you think Finland is a wealthy country? Give reasons for your answer.
- **b** Do you think life expectancy is good in Finland? Give reasons for your answer.
- **c** What does Professor Helliwell mean when he says, 'It's not about Finnish DNA'?
- **d** Why do you think students enjoy school and do so well?
- **e** What can you say about the Finns' sense of community?

Key words: Economics

GDP (Gross Domestic Product)
healthcare
income
life expectancy
per capita (Latin for 'each person')
population
social support
wealth

3 **Work in small groups.**

Other countries in the top 12 of the World Happiness Report

Costa Rica	Canada	Iceland
Denmark	New Zealand	Switzerland

- Each person is going to choose a country from the list above and do some research on it.

Research

Population — Life expectancy — Education
GDP per capita — What makes life good there?
Did you know? *(Find one or two interesting facts.)*

- Ask and answer questions about the country you have chosen:

What's the population of Iceland?
What's the life expectancy of people there?
What's education like there?

3.6 Be happy!

In this lesson you will...

- find out about a school where lessons to promote happiness are part of the school day
- use the present continuous passive to talk about activities at your own school.

- **Can happiness be taught? Could it be part of the school timetable?**

Reading

1 **Read the text. Do you agree with what Julia Annas says?**

According to the philosopher Julia Annas, 'Happiness is not a matter of the stuff you have, or whether you are beautiful, healthy, powerful or rich. A happy life is not one in which you just have these things – after all, plenty of people have all these things but in no way live happily.'

What Julia Annas says is based on the definition of happiness by the Greek philosopher Aristotle, who said happiness was doing well and living well.

Listening

22

2 **Listen to these students at a school where lessons to promote students' happiness are being added to the school day. How do they feel about their extra lessons?**

3 **Listen again and look at the chart. Which three activities is each person doing or going to do this term?**

a Aran b Prija c David

Sport and exercise	Creative activities	Cultural development/skills
ballet badminton basketball football development running self-defence advanced swimming table tennis volleyball	art appreciation drama ceramics choir circus skills creative writing guitar group origami painting	astronomy book club chess computer programming debating society handwriting robotics learning another language

Use of English Present continuous passive

Present reference

Lessons to promote happiness and well-being ***are being added*** *to the school day.*

Courses in Russian ***aren't being offered*** *this term. But they'll start next term.*

Are *students* ***being given*** *the chance to do activities outside normal classroom subjects?*
Yes, they are. / No, they aren't.

Future reference

Courses in Tai Chi ***are being introduced*** *next term.*

4 Complete the sentences using the present continuous passive.

- a introduce A longer day ***is being introduced***.
- b build A new science block …………..
- c offer This term courses in cooking and woodwork …………..
- d encourage We ………….. to learn to play a musical instrument.
- e extend ………….. the music room ………….. so that it can be used for concerts?
- f not use The school hall ………….. for exams this year because it isn't big enough.

Speaking

5 Work in pairs. Use the present continuous passive to answer the questions.

What's happening at your school at the moment? What about the future?

The science block is being repainted.

We are being encouraged to take up a new sport next term.

6 Work in groups. Discuss these questions.

- a Why do you think that, at some schools, students are being encouraged to do the kinds of activities in the list in Exercise 3?
- b What sort of sports, creative and cultural activities are being offered at your school at the moment?
- c If you were at the same school as Aran, David and Prija, which activities would you choose? Give your reasons.
- d What makes people of your age happy? Does this change as you get older?

3.7 Improve your writing

In this lesson you will...

- write a letter to the town council.

In your English class, you're discussing ideas for improving your local neighbourhood. Your teacher has asked you to send your suggestions to the head of your town council.

1 **Work in groups. Identify the things that could be improved in your local area. Then discuss what could be done and make a list.**

- planting trees and flowers
- improving street lighting
- designing posters and leaflets about protecting the environment
- reducing the speed limit near the school

2 **Decide on the three or four most important items on the list.**

3 **Plan your own letter.**

Step 1: Organise your ideas. Follow the structure of the model letter on the opposite page.

Step 2: Write a draft.

Step 3: Check your draft carefully for spelling, grammar and punctuation.

Step 4: Check your writing.

- Have you introduced yourself and started with something positive?
- Have you put each suggestion in a separate paragraph?

Step 5: Write the final version.

Writing tip

To end a formal letter if you don't know the name of the person, use 'Yours faithfully'. You can use 'Yours sincerely' if you know the name of the person you're writing to.

Which suggestion in the letter does this photo illustrate?

1 If you don't know the name of the person you're writing to, use 'Sir / Madam'.

2 Start by introducing yourself and say why you're writing.

3 Begin with something positive.

4 Identify the first problem and say what you would do about it.

5 Identify the problems in turn, starting a new paragraph for each of them. Give your suggested solution for each one.

6 If you want to ask a direct question, it's more polite to use the passive form rather than the active form. (Don't say 'Are you including cycleways and footpaths in the plans?')

7 'We look forward to hearing from you' is a useful phrase at the end of a formal letter.

Dear Sir/Madam,

We are students in Year 8 at City High School. In our English class, we're doing a project on the local community. We're being asked to come up with ideas to improve our neighbourhood.

It's a lively neighbourhood with some parks and green spaces. It's got shops, cafés and other places where you can buy food. However, this can cause a problem.

There is a lot of litter in the streets. We'd like to hand out some leaflets asking people to take their litter home with them instead of throwing it on the ground. At the same time, we'd like to do a litter collection and collect plastic bottles for recycling.

Another idea we've had is to paint the benches in the children's play area in the park next to our school. The benches are just grey concrete at the moment. They make the park look quite drab. We think it would be better if people had some nice, colourful benches to sit on.

Several of us catch the local train to school. We've noticed that the stations aren't very attractive. We'd like to plant some plants and flowers to make people feel happier when they're waiting at the station. If we did that, we would, of course, take turns to look after the plants and water them.

Finally, we know that a new road system for the centre of town is being considered at the moment. Are cycleways and footpaths being included in the plans? We hope so, because we want to encourage students to walk or cycle to school rather than coming in a car and causing congestion and pollution.

We look forward to hearing from you.

Yours faithfully,

Year 8 students

3.8 Project challenge

Project 1: Design a mural

You're going to design a mural for your local park.

1 Work in groups. Look carefully at the mural in the photo. What does it show? What do the shapes and colours suggest to you? Does the mural have a message? Why is it in a park?

2 Decide where your mural is going to be.

3 Discuss the size and shape of the mural.

4 What is the mural going to show? Is it going to have a message?

5 Ask students who are good at drawing to sketch your ideas for the mural. Make comments as they are sketching.

6 Produce a finished sketch of your mural.

7 Show your sketch to other groups and ask them to answer questions about it:

- What do you think of it?
- What do you think it shows?
- Do you think it has a message?
- Is there anything about it you'd change?

- How did working in groups help? How did you divide the tasks?
- When you asked other groups questions about your mural, did you agree with their comments?

Project 2: Plan an event

You're going to organise an event to raise money for a school trip.

1 First, read the plan for a leaflet produced by students at Woodford Academy.

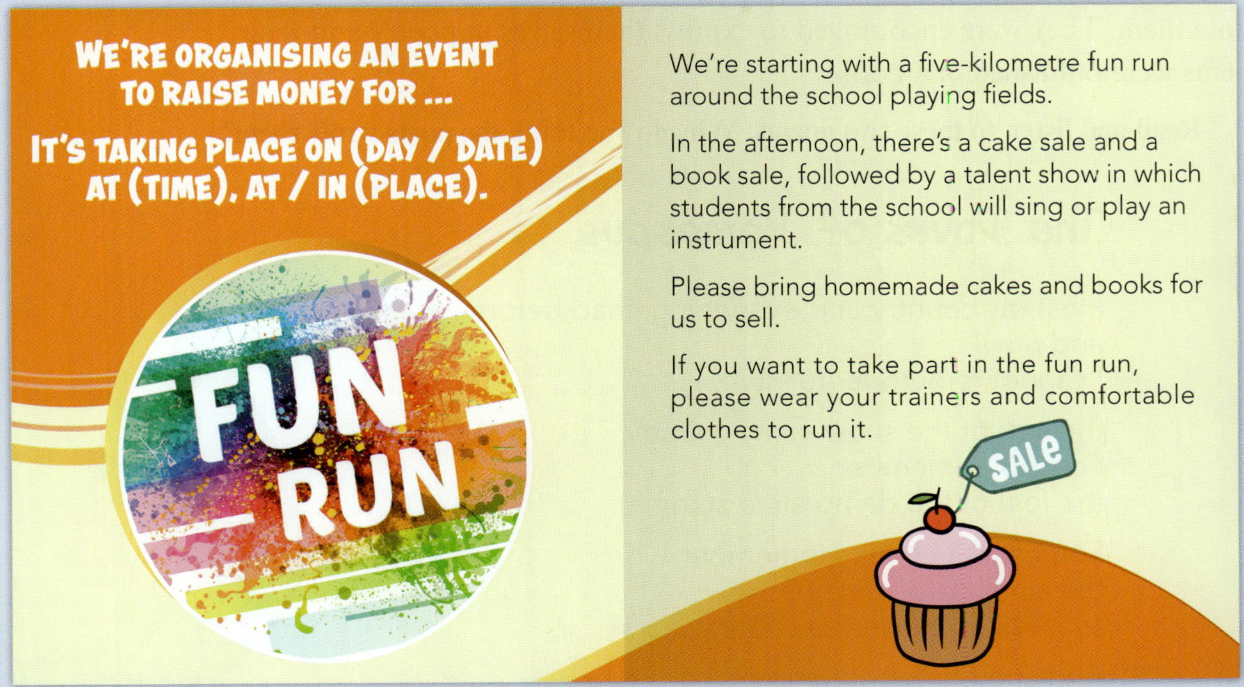

2 Work in groups. Decide on the event you're going to raise money for.

3 Decide on a date, time and place.

4 Share ideas about what your event will include. Here are some suggestions.

a cake sale	a raffle
a book sale	a sponsored event (a walk or a run)
a fun run	a talent show
a concert	a fashion show
a school sports day (school Olympics)	a treasure hunt

5 Decide what you'll need to prepare for the event. Are your plans realistic? Do you want to change any of them?

6 Produce a leaflet similar to the one above about your event.

- How did you decide which were the best ideas for the event?
- What did you learn from producing the leaflet for the event?

3.9 Poetry

The poems on these pages were written by students whose first language is not English. The students were all at the same school in Oxford when they wrote them. They were encouraged to express themselves in poetry and their poems were published in a book.

1 **Read and listen to these two poems. Why do you think the poets wrote them?**

The Doves of Damascus

I lost my country and everything I had before.
and now
I cannot remember for sure

the soft of the snow in my country,
I cannot remember
the feel of the damp air in summer.

Sometimes I think I remember
the smell of jasmine
as I walked down the street.

And sometimes autumn
with its orange and scarlet leaves
flying in the high Damascus sky.

And I am sure I remember
my grandmother's roof-garden,
its vines, its sweet red grapes,

the mint she grew in crates for tea.
I remember the birds, the doves
of Damascus. I remember

how they scattered.
I remember
trying to catch them.

Ftoun Abou Kerech (14)

2 **Answer these questions about 'The Doves of Damascus'.**

a What are the things Ftoun can't remember?

b What are the things she thinks she remembers?

c What are the things she's sure she remembers?

d Why do you think some of the memories are stronger than others?

e Which senses feature in Ftoun's memories?

The Return

No smell of fruit and marble floors, no
swirling noises of fans, no
animals, nothing
that felt alive.

No clear water, springs, no
fresh fruit high off the trees.
No huge balconies on top
of even higher houses where
we could laze around in the sun –
nothing of the sort, here.

The first noise back was the key in the lock.
The start of my updated life.

Maah-Noor Ali (15)

3 Answer these questions about 'The Return'.

- **a** There is a contrast between two places in the poem. What are these places?
- **b** Which senses feature in Maah-Noor's poem?
- **c** Which word occurs six times in the poem? Why?
- **d** Why do you think the poem is called 'The Return'?
- **e** We often use the word 'updated' in business and in digital contexts; for example, we talk of a computer software 'update'. Why do you think Maah-Noor chooses the word 'updated' in the final line to describe her new life?

4 Compare the two poems. Answer these questions.

- **a** What do the poems have in common?
- **b** Which images from the natural world do they include?
- **c** Which images from the manufactured world do they include?
- **d** At which point in each poem do we know that the poet has had to leave the country where they grew up?
- **e** What do the poems tell you about memories?

25 **5 Read and listen to 'I Shall Go Back'. What is the poem about?**

I Shall Go Back

I shall put the suitcase full of gifts
I have promised, down on the floor.
The gifts they have been waiting for.
I shall see their smiles.

I shall hang the flowers
that my cousins, uncles, and aunties
have put around my neck at the airport,
on the nail.

I shall sit down for dinner,
with family
and breathe the steam of *Quadid*
that nourishes you just by its smell.

I shall sleep outside,
in the hot summer night
and feel the soft winds holding me
and I shall never
wake up with the fear of war.

I shall hear my mum swooshing the carpet-sweeper
early in the morning.
I shall hear her say: *Wake up, guests
are coming. The house needs to be tidy.*

I shall feel at home, once again.

Shukria Rezaei (16)

Language tip

Shall is stronger than *will*. It suggests a serious commitment to do something.

6 Read the poem again and answer these questions.

- a What scene does Shukria describe in the first verse?
- b Who does she mention in the first three verses and why?
- c What is important about the food she mentions in lines 11 and 12?
- d What do you learn about the country she comes from in lines 13 to 15?
- e Which two lines in the poem suggest that Shukria's life hasn't always been happy?
- f How is this poem similar to the two poems on the previous pages?
- g What do you notice about the first line of each verse in this poem?
- h Why do you think Shukria wrote this poem?

7 Write your own poem about childhood memories. You can include these lines.

Sometimes I think I remember … I am sure I remember … I cannot remember for sure …

Check your progress

General knowledge quiz

How much do you remember about what you've learned?

1 Where is this?

2 What is a mural?

3 What do you call people from Finland: Finlanders, Finches or Finns?

4 What's the capital of Finland?

5 What does GDP stand for?

6 What does 'per capita' mean?

7 Complete Finland's nickname: 'The Land of the ..... Sun.'

8 Their Latin name is *aurora borealis* and they are coloured lights that appear in the night sky over parts of Scandinavia and the Arctic Circle. What's another name for them?

9 Who was Aristotle?

10 What is origami?

Vocabulary

1 **Use the information in the first sentence to complete the second sentence with one word.**

a It's a tall building with several apartments in it. It's a very nice apartment ***block***.

b No cars are allowed in this area of the city centre. It's the only car-......... zone in the city.

c You'll find lots of different shops, all in one building. It's a fantastic shopping ....

2 **Use a word from each column to complete each sentence.**

community	spaces
green	money
raise	problems
social	spirit

a We're trying to .... to build a swimming pool at school.

b The area once had lots of .... like gangs, crime and poor life expectancy.

c People here work together to try to improve the neighbourhood. There's a real sense of ....

d There are small play areas for children and there's a leisure centre, but there aren't many .... in my city.

Use of English

1 **Use the words in the three columns to make sentences, putting the verb in brackets in the correct form.**

a It's a lovely beach but you wouldn't be able to get there **b** He wouldn't get there on time **c** They wouldn't be able to buy a penthouse overlooking the sea **d** You wouldn't work in a zoo **e** I wouldn't ask for help	unless	I really (*need*) it. they (*be*) millionaires. you (*have*) a boat. you (*like*) animals. he (*take*) the first train at 5.00 a.m.

2 **Use the words in brackets to write a sentence that means the same as the first sentence(s).**

a I'd really like to walk to school. I don't like coming by car. (*instead of*)
I'd really like to walk to school instead of coming by car.

b 'Why don't you have a book sale?' said the teacher. (*suggest*)

c You can't do well in an exam if you don't revise. (*without*)

d Do you want to go to the cinema on Friday evening? (*feel like*)

e Would you like to join the photography club? (*be interested in*)

3 **Complete the second sentence so that it means the same as the first.**

a They aren't showing the film on TV until next year.
The film ***isn't being shown on TV until next year.***

b People are watching you.
You ....

c They're painting the school hall.
The school hall ....

d They're printing the leaflets at the moment.
The leaflets ....

Summary checklist

I can

- ☐ talk about what can be done to improve the quality of life in a neighbourhood.
- ☐ compare city life and country life and say where I would like to live.
- ☐ understand students talking about activities at school to promote happiness and well-being.
- ☐ write a letter to the town council with my ideas for improving the local area.
- ☐ plan a charity event and write a leaflet about it.

4 Advertising

In this unit you will…

- **learn** and **use** vocabulary to talk about advertising
- **read** about and **analyse** three advertisements
- **describe** and **discuss** an advert
- **listen** to and **analyse** a report about the psychology behind supermarket layouts
- **discuss** the success of a well-known brand
- **role-play** conversations about adverts on a school noticeboard
- **write** an advertisement
- **present** a plan for an outing, an activity or an improvement to the school recreation area
- **read** an extract from a classic story of American fiction
- **write** the dialogue for a story.

Getting started

**“How do you think advertising affects you?
Do you or your family buy things because you’ve seen adverts for them?
What kind of things?”**

Watch this!

4.1 Three for the price of two!

In this lesson you will...

- learn and use vocabulary to talk about advertising
- use prepositions preceding nouns in sales language.

- **Where do you see advertisements?**

Vocabulary

1 **Read the text. Think of an advertisement you've seen today. Where was it? What was it for?**

> **Advertising** is all around us. **Digital marketing** experts estimate that we see, on average, 4000 **advertisements** each day. They appear as **pop-ups** on our screens or **adverts** on TV, sometimes with a famous person to give them **celebrity endorsement**. Or you might see them on your way to school on **hoardings** and on big screens in the street. You read advertising **slogans** on the back of buses and on carrier bags. **Electronic ads** flash up at the side of the pitch during a match at a sports stadium. Big companies want their customers to buy their **products** rather than their competitors' products. They know who their **target audience** is and they want to create **brand loyalty** so that customers don't just buy their products once but continue to buy them. They spend a lot of money on **advertising campaigns**. They advertise through **social media**, through traditional **print media** and on television and at the cinema. Adverts appear in newspapers and in magazines.

2 **Which of the words or phrases in the text mean the following?**

a a new window that opens quickly on a computer screen in front of what you're working on ***pop-up***

b a famous person appearing in an ad saying they use and like a product

c a very large board on which advertisements are shown beside a road

d a short, easily remembered phrase, especially one used to advertise something

e the people a company expects will buy a particular product

f when people buy the same product from the same manufacturer or supplier rather than buying similar products

Speaking

3 Work in pairs. Discuss the questions.

- a How many different types of advertising have you seen or heard recently?
- b Can you think of any ads that have celebrity endorsement?
- c Can you think of examples of ads you've seen via social media, on TV, at the cinema or in magazines?
- d Think of a well-known advert. Who is the target audience for this ad? How is the ad trying to create brand loyalty?
- e How many advertising slogans can you think of?

Language tip

Ad, *advert* and *advertisement* all mean the same thing. *Ad* and *advert* are less formal than *advertisement*.

Listening

4 Listen to these adverts. Where would you hear them?

5 Listen to each of the adverts again. Which items are on offer in each of the following sections?

- a bakery
- b health and beauty
- c household and cleaning
- d soft drinks
- e frozen food

Use of English Prepositions preceding nouns

Today we have a special offer of three loaves of bread ***for*** *the* ***price*** *of two.*
(for = preposition; price = noun)

6 Complete the details of the offers with the correct prepositions. Then listen again and check.

at	for
on (x2)	to
up	

- a This offer is .... one week only, on all dental products.
- b Did you know that this week you can get .... 10% off all your household and cleaning items?
- c The soft drinks are .... sale in aisle number 6.
- d We have delicious frozen desserts .... offer this week, ... half price.

7 Adverts use persuasive language. Listen to the adverts again. Which words and phrases are used to persuade you to buy each item? For example, look at the underlined words in these sentences.

Today we have a <u>special</u> offer.

This is a <u>limited</u> offer, so … <u>Hurry!</u>

4.2 Three advertisements

In this lesson you will...

- read about and analyse three advertisements
- use the past participle with a passive meaning.

Key words: Media studies

brand identity
copyright
logo
permission

- **Think of advertisements you've seen. Why do you remember them?**

Reading

1 **Look at the first advertisement and read about it. How old is it?**

This is an advertisement for the Liu family needle shop in Jinan, Shandong Province, China. It is thought to be one of the earliest examples of printed advertising. Dating from the time of the Song Dynasty (960–1279), it shows an image of a rabbit, an early example of a logo. The words in the advertisement read: 'Jinan Liu's Fine Needle Shop … We make fine quality needles, to be ready for use at home in no time.'

2 **Answer the questions.**

a Why do you think the Liu family used the image of a rabbit as a logo on their leaflet?

b Why do you think the Liu family printed leaflets to advertise their needles?

3 **Look at the second advertisement. When do you think the picture was painted?**

This painting, originally known as *A Child's World*, became famous when it was used in an advertisement for Pears soap. The picture, painted by Sir John Everett Millais in 1886, shows his grandson. The painting and the copyright were then sold in 1887 to the director of Pears Soap for £2,200. He requested permission from Millais to alter the painting by adding a bar of Pears soap in the foreground, so that it could be used for advertising. The painting became known simply as *Bubbles*. Millais was one of the most popular artists in Britain at the time and the advertisement was hugely successful. However, Millais was criticised for allowing his painting to be used as an advert for soap. As he no longer owned the copyright, there was nothing he could do about it.

4 **Answer the questions.**

- **a** Why do you think the director of Pears Soap bought this particular picture to advertise his soap?
- **b** Why do you think the artist was criticised for allowing his painting to be used in an advertisement?

5 **Look at the third advertisement. When do you think it first appeared? Read about it.**

During the 1940s, the Coca-Cola company persuaded the US army that soldiers serving in other countries needed to drink Coca-Cola to keep their spirits up. It became a worldwide symbol of American culture – the best-selling soft drink in the world. The design of the bottle, the use of strong colour and the distinctive lettering created a brand identity still recognised today.

6 **Answer the questions.**

- **a** The Coca-Cola company wanted US soldiers in other countries to drink Coca-Cola 'to keep their spirits up'. Do you think there was another reason?
- **b** Why do you think Coca-Cola has used the same lettering and colours for over a hundred years?
- **c** What are your views about the advertising of products like Coca-Cola? How does it affect people's lives? Who does it benefit?

Use of English Present and past simple passive

To make both the present passive and the past passive you use a **past participle**:

*It **is thought** to be one of the earliest examples of printed advertising.*

*The painting **was used** in an advertisement for Pears soap.*

A clause is part of a sentence. Notice a clause beginning with a past participle has a passive meaning:

clause beginning with a past participle

*The picture, **painted** by Sir John Everett Millais in 1886, shows his grandson. (The picture **was painted** by Sir John Everett Millais in 1886.)*

*The design of the bottle, the use of strong colour and the distinctive lettering created a brand identity still **recognised** today. (The brand identity **is** still **recognised** today.)*

clause beginning with a past participle

How are these sentences combined in the text about Pears soap?

This painting became famous when it was used in an advertisement for Pears soap.
The painting was originally known as *A Child's World*.

4.3 The more you look ...

In this lesson you will...

- listen to opinions about an advert and compare them with your own
- describe and discuss an advert.

- **Look at the two adverts on these pages. What are your first impressions?**

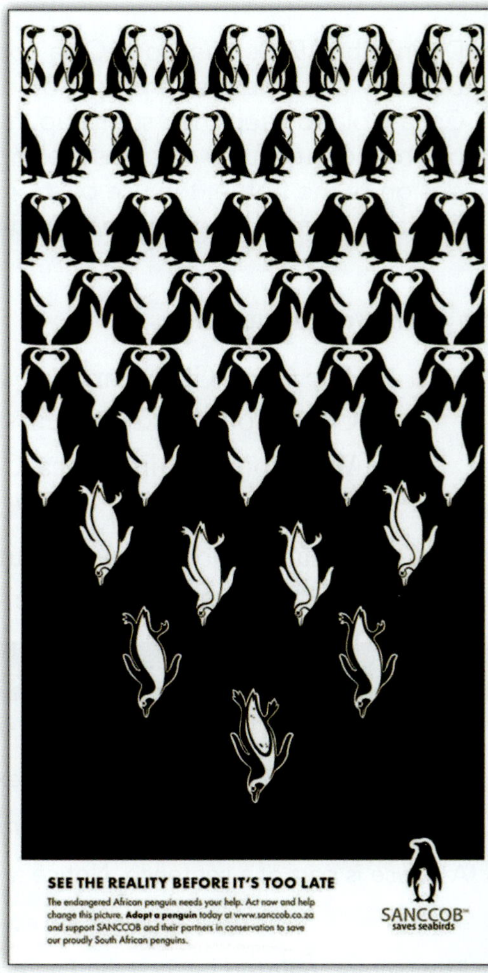

Listening and speaking

27

1 **Listen to two people talking about the first advert. Did they have the same ideas as you?**

2 **Listen again and complete the conversation with the words from the list.**

Adjectives	Nouns
artistic	detail
clever	message
effective	optical illusion (a picture that tricks your brain)
fascinating	pattern
memorable	shapes
simple	work of art
striking	

A: What do you think of this ad?

B: I like it. I think it's really ....[1].

A: Yes, it's ....[2] and it's only in black and white. It's a kind of ....[3]. The more you look at it, the more you see.

B: When I first looked at it, I saw a ....[4]. I didn't look at the ....[5]. Then I looked at the top line and saw it was a line of penguins.

A: And then your eyes go further down and you see how it changes. You see that the white ....[6] between the pairs of penguins have become penguins themselves.

B: Yes, and they seem to be diving down into a black space.

A: Do you think it's meant to be water – the ocean, or something like that?

B: I don't know.

A: You try to understand what the picture is telling you. You see the ....[7] at the bottom of the picture and then you get it! It's about penguins being in danger of extinction.

B: Why do you think it's so ....[8]?

A: I suppose because it's very ....[9]. It's like a ....[10], like a painting in black and white.

B: And it takes time to work out what it means. It's very ....[11]. It draws you in because you can't understand it immediately. That's what makes it ....[12] and ....[13].

3 **These phrases all occur in the conversation. Can you explain them in your own words?**

a The more you look, the more you see.

b And then you get it!

c It's meant to be (water).

28

4 **Work in groups. Talk about the advert below. Use the conversation in Exercise 2 and these words to help you: *lollipop, ants, path, grass.* You can also listen to a conversation about the advert.**

5 **In your groups, compare the two adverts. How are they similar? How are they different? In your opinion, which one is more effective?**

4.4 The psychology of shopping

In this lesson you will...

- listen to and analyse a report about the psychology behind supermarket layouts
- use reflexive pronouns.

- **Have you ever thought about the way supermarkets are designed? For example, why are the fresh fruit and vegetables usually close to the entrance?**

Vocabulary and listening

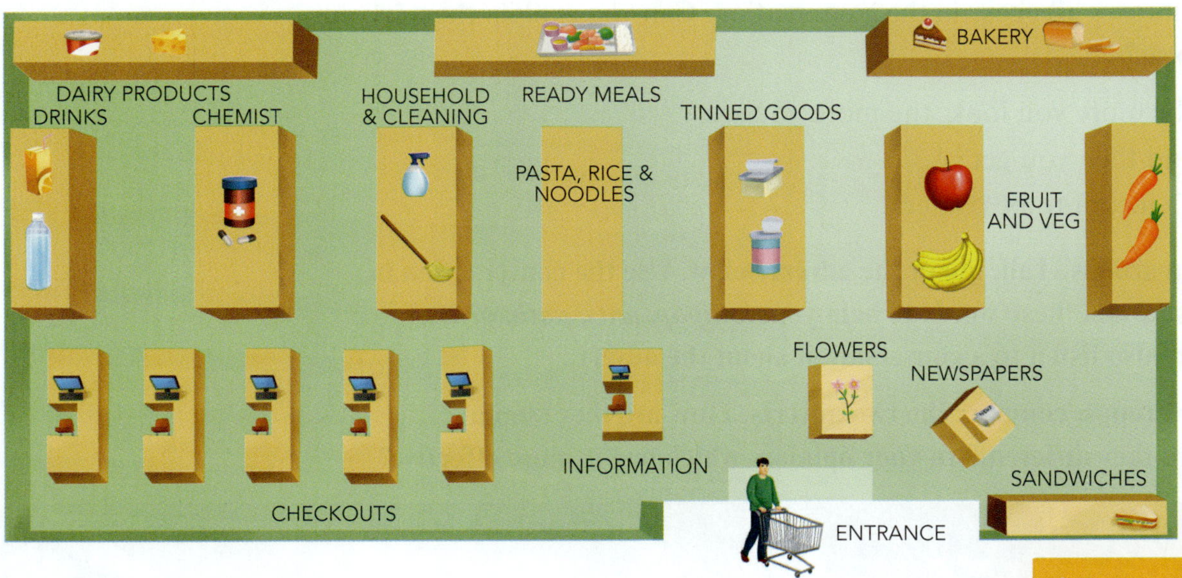

29

1 **Listen. Which sections of the diagram does the radio programme mention?**

2 **Listen again and match the words to the definitions.**

1	checkout	a	important things that you need
2	squashed	b	a large metal basket on wheels used for carrying shopping
3	trolley	c	passages for customers to walk along in a supermarket
4	essentials	d	pressed into a flat shape, sometimes causing damage
5	resist	e	stop yourself doing something that you want to do
6	tempting	f	the place in the supermarket where you pay
7	aisles	g	to have earned something because of good (or bad) behaviour
8	deserve	h	very attractive, making you want it

Language tip

shelf (singular)
shelves (plural)

aisle is pronounced like *I'll*

3 Listen again and discuss these questions.

a Why are the fruit and vegetables near the door?

b Why is the bakery section at the back of the store?

c Why do you have to pass the ready-meals sections to get to the water?

d Why are there little bars of chocolate and similar items near the checkout?

e The reporter was asked to do a report on the layout of a typical supermarket. Is it simply a factual account or can you tell what he thinks about supermarkets? Give reasons for your answers.

Use of English Reflexive pronouns

The reflexive pronouns are: *myself, yourself, himself, herself, itself, ourselves, yourselves, themselves.*

We use reflexive pronouns with verbs when the object is the same person (or thing) as the subject.

*You help **yourself** to what you want.*

We also use reflexive pronouns to emphasise the subject or object.

*You can even weigh them **yourself**.*

4 Complete the sentences with the correct reflexive pronouns.

a You can help *yourself* to a free sample of cheese at our dairy counter.

b I'm going to make .... a nice stir-fry with these fresh noodles.

c Can you pack your things .... ? Or do you need any help?

d Ali and Sara, stop playing with that trolley! You'll hurt ....

e We always treat .... to a nice dessert at the weekend.

f Most customers like to choose their fruit and vegetables ....

Speaking

5 Work in groups. Talk about your local supermarket.

a Does your supermarket follow the pattern of the typical supermarket described in the radio report?

b Does your supermarket often have special offers? Give examples.

c How does it make you want to buy things?

d What do you think about supermarkets? What are the advantages? What are the disadvantages?

4.5 The creation of a brand

Key words: Business studies

- a global luxury brand
- a marketing campaign
- an exclusive image
- to go into business (with)
- to manufacture

In this lesson you will...

- read an article about the history of the polo shirt
- discuss the success of a well-known brand.

- **What are the big brand names in clothing today? How many of them are sports brands?**

Reading

1 **Read the article. Why is René Lacoste's name remembered today?**

2 **Choose a sentence to complete each paragraph in the article.**

a Polo players, for example, swapped their long-sleeved, heavy cotton shirts for Lacoste's short-sleeved shirts and gave the shirt its name – the polo shirt.

b It has even become a standard item of school uniform throughout the world.

c Lacoste had the crocodile embroidered onto his blazer, which he wore to matches.

d It was made of soft cotton and was comfortable, light and cool.

e Men wore long-sleeved white shirts, white trousers and ties, and women wore ankle-length, long-sleeved dresses and hats.

Speaking

3 **Work in pairs. Take turns to ask each other one question on each paragraph in the text. For example:**

Paragraph 1
Partner A: Who played tennis in the 19th and early 20th centuries?
Partner B: The upper and middle classes. How were tennis players expected to look?
Partner A: Very smart and formal.

Paragraph 2
Partner A: What happened …?

4 **Work in small groups.**

a What do the words in the business studies key words box mean? Find them in the text.

b Each student should write three key points which, in their opinion, made Lacoste a successful brand.

c Share your ideas. Use the phrases in the business studies key words box in your discussion.

The history of the polo shirt

In the 19th and early 20th centuries, tennis was very much a sport of the upper and middle classes. Tennis players were expected to look very smart and formal. **[1]** .....

Then, in 1926, at the US Open Championship, the French tennis player René Lacoste wore a shirt which he himself had designed. It created a sensation. Instead of having long sleeves that the players wore rolled up, the Lacoste shirt had short sleeves and a collar that could be turned up to protect the neck from the sun. **[2]** .....

The same year, Lacoste's friend, Robert George, drew him a picture of a crocodile with its mouth open. This was because Lacoste was known as 'The Crocodile' by his fans, due to his tenacity on court. **[3]** .....

In 1933, André Gillier, the owner of a large clothing factory in France, went into business with Lacoste and began to manufacture the short-sleeved Lacoste shirt with the crocodile logo on it. The shirts soon became popular with tennis players and other sportspeople. **[4]** .....

Until 1950, clothes for tennis were only made in white, but in 1951 Lacoste had the idea of expanding his range to include shirts in a variety of colours. According to the slogan of the marketing campaign, polo shirts were 'the status symbol of the competent sportsman'. The Lacoste polo shirts, sold only in the most expensive shops and department stores, established Lacoste as a global luxury brand with an exclusive image. Nowadays, the polo shirt is a classic item of 'smart casual' dress. It's more formal than a T-shirt but less formal than a long-sleeved shirt. **[5]** .....

created a sensation: caused a lot of excitement, surprise or interest

tenacity: determination to do something, even if it takes a long time and is difficult

embroidered: decorated by sewing small patterns or pictures in coloured thread (onto a piece of cloth)

blazer: a smart jacket, often worn as part of school uniform or by members of a sports club

swapped: exchanged

standard: accepted as normal

4.6 For sale

In this lesson you will...

- role-play conversations about adverts on a school noticeboard
- use compound adjectives.

- **If you have things at home that you don't use or don't need any more, what should you do with them?**

Reading

1 **Read the adverts on the school noticeboard. Which is the odd one out? Why?**

1

Baseball boots

Multicoloured baseball boots. Never worn. Reason for sale: too small.

2

Tabletop football game

Hardly used tabletop football game, in original box!

3

Children's book

A book of bedtime stories. Classic stories from all over the world. Would suit a younger brother or sister!

4

Wanted

Kind, patient animal lover wanted to look after my well-behaved cat for two weeks while I'm on holiday.

5

Games console

Games console with set of six family-friendly, skill-building games. In good condition.

2 **Which extra piece of information goes with each advert?**

a Food and own bed provided.
b Will provide long-lasting fun for football fans of all ages!
c Size 35; white laces
d With individual and multiplayer options.
e Beautiful pictures and in very good condition.

Use of English Compound adjectives

You can use two words together to make a compound adjective.

well-behaved	*A **well-behaved** cat.*
multicoloured	*A pair of **multicoloured** baseball boots.*

The two words in a compound adjective are sometimes joined, sometimes hyphenated and sometimes written as two separate words.

Writing tip

In short adverts, we often write in note form rather than in full sentences.

3 **Look at these compound adjectives from the adverts. What do they mean?**

a multicoloured (baseball boots) ***having many colours***
b hardly used, tabletop (table football game)
c well-behaved (cat)
d family-friendly, skill-building (video games)
e long-lasting (fun)

Writing

4 **Write out each advertisement in Exercise 1 using full sentences.**

*1 **These multicoloured baseball boots have never been worn. The reason for selling them is that they are too small. The boots are size 35 and they have white laces.***

Listening and speaking

30 5 **Work in pairs. Listen to the conversation about the first advert. Then role-play conversations about each of the items in the other adverts. One is the person who has placed the ad and the other is the person who is interested in it.**

4.7 Improve your writing

In this lesson you will...

- write an advertisement.

1 **Advertisements use persuasive techniques to influence the way you think and feel. Find an example of each of the following techniques in the adverts on the opposite page.**

a A short message that is easy to remember, sometimes using alliteration (words that start with the same sound or letter).

b Imperatives: verb forms that tell you to do something.

c Exaggerating the qualities of something, often using superlatives, for example *the cleanest wash*, *the most fantastic experience.*

d Strong adjectives for emphasis in descriptions, for example *wonderful*, *marvellous*.

e Personal pronouns to address the reader directly and involve them in the ad: *you*, *we*, etc.

f Pictures or photos that make the reader feel an emotion.

g Words that are used to make the reader feel an emotion such as *happiness*, *sadness*, *excitement*, *love*.

h Repetition of words or ideas to make the advert memorable.

2 **Work in pairs. Did you find the same the examples?**

3 **Write an advertisement for a food product or a holiday. Use the ideas below and the model texts to help you. Use some of the persuasive techniques from the list in Exercise 1.**

A fruit drink

healthy

refreshing

vitamin-rich

recyclable bottle

Family holiday

award-winning

luxury log cabin

snorkelling, scuba diving, surfing

island boat trips

Try our Tip-top Tasty Treat. This high-energy bar, made from organic fruit and nuts, contains only natural sugars. You'll love it. It's the tastiest, nuttiest, healthiest bar you can eat and it'll make you feel terrific! Go on, treat yourself!

AFRICAN SAFARI

BOOK ONLINE AT greatholidays4u.com

Take your family on a holiday to remember. Go on safari to see some of Africa's most amazing wildlife. Camp out in the desert under the clearest skies on the planet and see thousands of stars. Enjoy the comfort of a superb, five-star hotel with fantastic views over the national park. Then complete your perfect vacation with a relaxing three-day stay at the beach.

You and your family will love every moment of this trip. It'll be a holiday to remember.

4.8 Project challenge

Project 1: Create an advertisement

You are going to create an advertisement for a product.

1. Work in pairs. Look back at the advertisement for Pears soap in Lesson 4.2. Find a well-known painting, for example, *The Girl with the Pearl Earring*.
2. Think of a product you could advertise by adapting the painting. Remember how a bar of Pears soap was added to the painting by Millais.
3. What would you add to the picture? Would you add something visual? Would you add a logo? Would you add some text?
4. Write notes saying how you would adapt the picture.
   For example:
   - Add a … in the background.
   - Add some text in the bottom left corner of the picture.
5. Present your picture to the class and explain how you would adapt it using the notes you made. Ask the class for comments and other suggestions.

- What did you learn when you were looking for a painting to use?
- Did you find any of the class's suggestions useful? Why?

Project 2: Present a plan to an audience

You're going to present a plan for an outing, an activity or an improvement to the school recreation area.

Imagine your headteacher has asked your year group to give ideas for one of the following:

- a class outing to a place of interest
- a new after-school activity
- an item for the school recreation area.

1 Work in groups. Choose an idea and decide what you will propose for it.

2 Make a list of the reasons your idea should be accepted.

3 Write down key words and phrases to use when you present the idea. Remember to include persuasive language. (Look back at Lesson 4.7 to help you.) Include some compound adjectives where appropriate.

4 Write a plan for your presentation. Here are some points to help you.

- What questions can you ask to find out how to interest the audience in your idea?
- How will you explain your idea and why you have chosen it?
- What kind of arguments might the audience give against your idea and how will you think of positive responses?
- How will you finish your presentation in an interesting or amusing way?

5 Give your presentation.

6 As a class, evaluate each presentation by asking the following questions:

- Did we establish good communication with the audience?
- Did we explain our idea clearly?
- Did we persuade the audience to support our idea?
- Did we keep the audience's attention?
- How would you rate our presentation overall?

- What are the three most useful things you have learned from doing this project?
- How will your experience of doing this project help you in the future?

4.9 Fiction

The Adventures of Tom Sawyer by Mark Twain was published in 1876. It's a novel about a young boy growing up by the Mississippi river. It's set in the fictional town of St Petersburg, which is based on Hannibal, Missouri, in the USA, where Mark Twain lived.

1 In the preface to *The Adventures of Tom Sawyer,* Mark Twain said that although he had written the book for boys and girls, he hoped that adults would read it too. Why do you think some children's books also appeal to adults?

31 **2 Read and listen to the extract. Answer the questions.**

- a What do you learn about Aunt Polly?
- b What do you learn about Tom?
- c Why does Tom think the other boys will make fun of him? *(line 32)*
- d What is Tom's 'brilliant idea'? *(line 33)*
- e What does Ben think when he sees Tom painting the fence?
- f Why doesn't Tom let Ben paint at first?
- g Why was this a good day for everybody in the end?
- h What is the lesson that Tom learns?

3 Look at the underlined phrases in these sentences from the extract. Can you think of another way of saying them?

- a The trouble is, he makes me laugh. *(line 19)*
- b The other boys will make fun of me. *(line 32)*
- c I bet you'd like to come. *(line 37)*
- d It's a shame you have to work. *(line 38)*
- e I can't believe my eyes. *(line 78)*

[9] **closet:** American English for a cupboard built into the wall of a room

[30] **yard:** a unit of measurement (1 yard = 0.9144 metres)

[30] **feet:** *(singular foot)* a unit of measurement. There are three feet in one yard (1 foot = 0.3048 yards).

'Tom, where are you?'

No answer.

The old lady went to the door and looked out into the garden.

'Tom!'

There was a noise behind her, and she turned around just in time to catch the jacket of a small boy who was trying to run past her.

'There you are! Why were you in the closet? What were you doing?'

'Nothing, Aunt.'

'Nothing! What's that on your hands and your mouth? It's jam! You were eating my best jam!'

'Look behind you, Aunt!'

The old lady turned around quickly, and the boy escaped. He climbed the garden fence and disappeared.

'I never learn,' thought Aunt Polly. She smiled. 'The trouble is, he makes me laugh. And he's my own dead sister's boy, poor thing. I can't be too strict with him. But he should learn. Tomorrow's Saturday, and when all the other boys are having a holiday, Tom's going to paint the fence.'

* * *

It was a perfect summer morning, warm and sunny. The birds were singing, and everyone in St Petersburg was happy. Everyone except Tom. He was standing by the fence with a bucket of white paint and a paintbrush. The fence was thirty yards long and nine feet high. He started to paint. 'It's going to be a long job,' he thought, 'and all the other boys will make fun of me.'

Then he had an idea – a brilliant idea.

As Tom was painting, Ben Rogers came up the street. He was eating an apple.

'Hello, Tom,' he said. 'I'm going down to the river to go swimming. I bet you'd like to come. It's a shame you have to work.'

Tom's mouth watered for the apple, but he continued to paint. He stood back from the fence to admire his work, like an artist.

'Work?' said Tom. 'This isn't work. After all, you don't get the chance to paint a fence every day.'

Ben watched as Tom was painting. He became more and more interested.

'Tom, let me paint for a time.'

Tom thought about it. 'No, I'm afraid I can't,' he said. 'Aunt Polly wants me to do it, because she knows I'll do it so carefully.'

'Just let me do a little bit,' said Ben.

'Sorry,' said Tom.

'I'll give you some of my apple.'

'Sorry,' Tom repeated.

'I'll give you all of my apple!'

'Well,' said Tom after a pause, 'all right. But make sure you do a really good job.'

Tom sat down and ate the apple. As Ben was painting, Billy Fisher came by to laugh at Tom. But when he saw Ben, he too wanted to try painting, and, in exchange for his kite, Tom let him. Then Johnny Miller came by. And in exchange for a toy soldier, Tom let him paint too …

By the middle of the afternoon, the fence had three coats of paint on it, and Tom had a collection of all sorts of things.

Tom said to himself that it wasn't such a bad world after all. If you make something difficult to get, people will always want it. He went into the house.

'Can I go and play now, Aunt?' he asked.

'What, already? How much have you done?'

'All of it.'

'Don't lie to me, Tom.'

'I'm not lying, Aunt Polly.'

Aunt Polly went outside.

'Well, Tom!' she said. 'I can't believe my eyes. Yes, you can go and play. And you can have the best apple in the bowl.'

Adapted from *The Adventures of Tom Sawyer* by Mark Twain

Mark Twain's first idea was to write a play about the adventures of Tom Sawyer.

4 **Work in groups. You're going to present *The Adventures of Tom Sawyer* as a play.**

Mark Twain

a Look at the extract on page 95.

b Divide it into scenes like this:

Scene 1
A village cottage with a door looking out into the garden.
Characters: Tom, Aunt Polly.

Scene 2
Outside the cottage. Tom is starting to paint a wooden fence.
Characters: Tom, Ben Rogers, Billy Fisher, Johnny Miller

Scene 3
Inside the cottage
Characters: Tom, Aunt Polly

c Write the three scenes. You could start like this:

> **The Adventures of Tom Sawyer**
> **Scene 1**
> *A village cottage with a door looking out into the garden*
> TOM, AUNT POLLY
> Aunt Polly: Tom, where are you?
> Tom?
> *Aunt Polly looks out into the garden.*
> Aunt Polly: Tom!
> *Tom appears behind Aunt Polly with jam on his face and hands. He tries to run past Aunt Polly and out through the door, but she manages to catch hold of his jacket.*
> Aunt Polly: There you are! Why were you in the closet? What were you doing?

d Decide who is going to read each part. You need five actors and a narrator.

e You need other students to make sound effects like the birds singing.

f You will also need props. Make a list of them:
A bucket for the paint, a paintbrush, …

g Rehearse your scenes.

h Perform the scenes to the other members of the class.

Check your progress

General knowledge quiz

How much do you remember about what you've learned?

1 What is this and what does it show?

2 What is celebrity endorsement and why is it used in advertising?

3 What is the word for a short, easily remembered phrase used to advertise a product?

4 Who was Sir John Everett Millais and what is his connection with a bar of soap?

5 What was the relationship between the boy in the Pears soap ad and Sir John Everett Millais?

6 Millais could not stop his painting being used to advertise soap. Why?

7 What is the connection between the poster and the soldier in this picture?

8 What sport did René Lacoste play?

9 What name did his fans give him?

10 What item of clothing did he design?

Vocabulary

1 **Match the words from the two columns to make expressions used in advertising.**

a	digital	audience
b	celebrity	campaign
c	target	endorsement
d	brand	loyalty
e	advertising	marketing

2 **Write the word for each definition.**

a The section of a supermarket where bread is sold and sometimes baked.

b The place in a supermarket where you pay.

c The areas you walk along between the shelves in a supermarket.

d The large metal basket on wheels that you use to put your shopping in at the supermarket.

e The section of a supermarket where you find cheese, milk and yoghurt.

3 **Complete the text with the words from the list.**

art detail illusion pattern shapes

This ad is an optical ......[1]. At first you see a ......[2] in black and white and then, when you look at the ......[3], you realise that all the ......[4] are birds. It's based on a work of ......[5] by the Dutch graphic artist M.C. Escher.

Use of English

1 Choose the correct preposition.

a Buy three items *as / for* the price of two.

b Locally grown strawberries are *in / on* sale in the fruit and vegetable section.

c The offer is *for / on* one week only.

d Are the vegetarian ready meals *in / on* offer at the moment?

2 Combine the pairs of sentences using past participles. Follow the example.

a The films have been a great success. They are based on the books by J.K. Rowling.
The films, based on the books by J.K. Rowling, have been a great success.

b Our new fruit drinks are featured in the advertising campaign. They are made from mango, lime and cactus water.

c These watches are very expensive. They are sold only in the most exclusive shops.

d A simple leaflet was one of the earliest forms of printed advertising. It was printed over a thousand years ago.

3 Complete the sentences with the correct reflexive pronouns.

a Help .... to a free magazine.

b I bought .... a new shopping bag, so I don't use plastic bags any more.

c We treated .... to ice creams at the cinema.

d They were very surprised to see .... on the TV news.

e She made .... a sandwich.

4 Complete the adverts using words from the box to make compound adjectives.

coloured	known	friendly
painted	shaped	

a These limited-edition prints are all by well-........ artists.

b These brightly .... scarves are on sale at 50% of their original price.

c This beautiful hand-........ dish dates from the Ming Dynasty.

d This unusual egg-........ radio is also waterproof and can be used in the bathroom.

e This is a family-........ film which will appeal to adults and children.

Summary checklist

I can

- ☐ understand the detail of advertising campaigns for well-known products.
- ☐ discuss how supermarkets encourage shoppers to buy products on sale.
- ☐ understand an article about the history of a well-known clothing brand.
- ☐ write adverts for items to sell, a food product or a holiday.
- ☐ create an advertisement based on a well-known painting.
- ☐ present an idea to an audience.
- ☐ write the dialogue for three scenes from a story.

5 Natural resources

In this unit you will...

- **learn** about Costa Rica's natural resources and how they are used
- **make** predictions about how energy will be generated in the future
- **do** a quiz to find out how eco-aware you are
- **understand** and **use** detailed information about water
- **discuss** the importance of rainforests
- **role-play** a debate about the environment
- **write** an informative account about natural resources
- **write** a presentation about energy in your country
- **create** a poster for an environmental issue
- **read** speeches by an environmental campaigner
- **write** a short speech about an environmental issue.

Getting started

"What do you think of as natural resources? What are they used for and why are they important?"

Watch this!

5.1 A natural paradise

The Monteverde cloud forest, Costa Rica

In this lesson you will...

- learn about Costa Rica's natural resources and how they are used
- learn and use vocabulary to talk about renewable energy.

- **How do we generate energy for electricity and other types of power?**

Listening

1 **Before you listen, match the words in the vocabulary box to the definitions.**

ecologist	zero-carbon emissions	hydro-electric power
natural resources	renewable sources	source
eco-friendly policies	solar power	geothermal power
carbon-neutral		

a emissions producing no carbon dioxide
b a scientist whose work relates to the environment
c energy from heat in the ground
d energy from sunlight
e energy from water
f ideas that people agree are good for the environment
g materials or substances that are produced by the environment and can be used to provide energy, food and clothing
h sources that replace themselves, like water
i taking the same amount of carbon dioxide out of the air as you produce
j the place where something comes from

2 **Listen to the first part of an interview about Costa Rica. What does it focus on?**

Vocabulary

3 **Listen again. Use the words and phrases in Exercise 1 to give the main points of the first part of the interview.**

4 **Listen to the second part of the interview. Alicia, the ecologist, says that Costa Rica is a 'tropical paradise'. What would you expect to find in a 'tropical paradise'?**

5 **Listen again. Then answer the questions.**

- **a** What are cloud forests?
- **b** What can you find in the cloud forests?
- **c** Alicia speaks of the different 'species' of plants, animals and insects. What is another word for 'species'?
- **d** What shape and what colour are guanacaste trees?
- **e** What is a motmot?
- **f** What do you think biodiversity means?
- **g** Why do you think biodiversity could be seen as one of Costa Rica's most important natural resources?

Use of English Complex noun phrases 1

Before a noun, you can use:

- determiners (words like *the*, *a / an*, *this*, *some*, *any*, *every*) ***any*** *plants or animal species*
- quantifiers ***a lot of*** *rain*, ***most of*** *Costa Rica's energy*
- numbers ***six*** *volcanoes*
- adjectives *a* ***tropical*** *paradise*

Here are two examples from the interview you have just heard.

Every one of the *cloud forests is home to thousands of different species of animals, plants and insects.*

Costa Rica is ***one of the most biodiverse*** *countries on Earth.*

A colourful bird with a racket-shaped tail. What's it called?

6 **Use multiple adjectives to make sentences about your country.**

- **a** There aren't .... volcanoes / cloud forests / deserts.
- **b** .... country's energy comes from …
- **c** We have / We don't have .... rain.
- **d** There are .... national parks.
- **e** .... interesting places to visit in my country is …

Speaking

7 **Work in groups. Does your country have a national tree and a national bird? What are they? How would you describe them?**

As you are speaking, help each other to use expressions from the Use of English boxes such as 'one of the most …', and try to use two or three adjectives before a noun.

Use of English Complex noun phrases 2

The order of adjectives in a noun phrase

You can use several adjectives before a noun. Notice the order of adjectives:

It's a ***beautiful*** (opinion) ***brightly coloured*** (description) *bird.*

It's a ***huge*** (size), ***old*** (age), ***mushroom-shaped*** (shape), ***reddish-brown*** (colour) *tree.*

5.2 Generating energy

In this lesson you will...

- find out how energy is generated from different sources
- make predictions about how energy will be generated in the future.

- **Imagine a day without electricity. What would it be like?**

Reading

1 **Read the descriptions below of sources of energy. Which are renewable and which are non-renewable?**

2 **In the text about sources of energy, which of the following statements are true, which are false and which are implied?**

a You can only produce geothermal energy in volcanic areas. ***False***

b There are several ways of producing power from water.

c Nuclear waste can be dangerous.

d Wind turbines produce electricity.

e Photovoltaic cells rather than solar panels are used in large-scale solar farms.

f Fossil fuels can provide all the energy we need now and in the future.

g Electric cars don't produce carbon emissions.

Language tip

Implied meaning

If something is *implied*, it is suggested but not directly stated. For example:

Fossil fuels, like coal and oil, produce carbon emissions. We need to have zero carbon emissions by 2050.

This implies we have to stop using coal and oil by 2050.

Geothermal energy

In volcanic areas, radioactive substances in the rock, such as uranium, release geothermal energy underground. This forces water and steam to the surface, which is used to drive generators. In non-volcanic areas, where there are hot rocks underground but no water, a pump forces cold water into the ground. It then rises as hot water and steam.

Hydro-electric power

Water can be used to generate energy in several ways. The movement of waves in the sea, a fast-flowing river, water coming down a waterfall and water released from a dam can all generate power.

Fossil fuels

Fossil fuels, like coal and oil, produce carbon emissions. Fossil fuels are limited resources: once they are all used up, they cannot be replaced. Gradually fossil fuels will be replaced by other sources of energy. There will be fewer cars with petrol and diesel engines while more and more electric vehicles will be made. In the EU, for example, cars with petrol or diesel engines will not be sold after 2030. The aim is to have zero carbon emissions from cars by 2050.

Speaking

3 **Work in groups. Discuss the advantages and disadvantages of the types of energy generation you've just read about. Use these words to help you. You can also use the words in the science key words box.**

Adjectives	Nouns	Verbs
clean / dirty	environment	pollute
safe / dangerous	global warming	provide
cheap / expensive	climate change	generate
reliable / unreliable	emissions	produce
renewable / non-renewable	carbon dioxide	

4 **Write sentences using the verbs in brackets in the future passive.**

- **a** By the middle of the century, most of the power we need ***will be produced*** (*produce*) from renewable sources.
- **b** The governments of several countries have said that no new coal-fired power stations .... (*build*).
- **c** We hope that by 2050, all electricity .... (*generate*) from renewable sources.
- **d** Solar energy .... (*export*) to countries that don't have a lot of sunlight.
- **e** In 50 years' time, fossil fuels .... (*not / use*) to produce electricity.
- **f** Charging points to recharge electric vehicles .... (*provide*) in car parks, motorway service stations and shopping centres.
- **g** Carbon emissions .... (*reduce*) if clean energy sources are used to replace fossil fuels.

Key words: Science

carbon dioxide
chemical reaction
nuclear fuels
plutonium
radioactive (substances / materials / waste)
uranium

Use of English Future passive

Use the future passive to make statements and give predictions about the future.

Gradually fossil fuels *will + be + past participle* ***will be replaced*** *by other sources of energy ...*

Cars with petrol or diesel engines ***will not be sold*** *after 2030 ...*

Nuclear fuels

The main nuclear fuels are uranium and plutonium. They are not burned to release energy; they produce energy through a chemical reaction in a nuclear reactor. The process does not produce carbon dioxide. However, radioactive material is dangerous and nuclear waste remains radioactive for thousands of years.

Wind power

The blades on a wind turbine are moved by the wind. This creates energy that drives a generator to produce electricity.

Solar power

Solar energy is produced either by solar cells or solar panels. Solar cells (photovoltaic cells) convert sunlight into electrical energy. Solar panels don't generate electricity; they heat water that is pumped through them. Countries such as China, India and the USA are installing large-scale solar farms so that more and more of their electricity will be produced from solar energy.

5.3 Test your eco-awareness!

In this lesson you will...

- do a quiz to find out how eco-aware you are
- discuss ways you can be eco-friendly in your daily life.

Language tip

Find these expressions in the quiz. Can you think of another way of saying the phrases in bold?

***It's all very well saying that**, but it's just not enough time.*

***It makes sense**, because two minutes is more than enough.*

***I haven't got a clue, I'm afraid**. I've never thought about it.* (Two expressions: *I haven't got a clue* and *I'm afraid*.)

- **What does it mean to be 'eco-aware'? What is an 'eco-friendly' product?**

Reading and listening

34 **1 Work in pairs. Read the quiz on the opposite page and listen to Amaya and Jamil doing it. Note down Jamil's answers. Look at the analysis. Is Jamil mostly a, b or c?**

Speaking

2 Work in pairs. Take turns to ask and answer the questions in the quiz. Make sure you pronounce these expressions correctly, with the stress in the correct places. (The main stress is marked in bold.)

- eco-a**ware**
- eco-**friend**ly
- solar-**pow**ered
- a solar-powered **char**ger
- geothermal **en**ergy
- CO_2 (the stress is on '2')
- carbon di**ox**ide
- energy-ef**fi**cient
- renewable **sour**ces
- solar **cells**

Writing

3 Work in small groups. Write two more questions with multiple-choice answers to add to the quiz. They can be serious or humorous. Here are some examples to help you:

What is biodiversity?
A It's when you study biology at university, I think.
B It's something to do with …
C …

How do you get to school every day?
A In a car of course!
B …
C …

What do you do to recycle or avoid using plastic? …
A …
B I take water to school in a reusable bottle.
C …

Speaking

4 **Work in small groups. Discuss these two questions.**

- a What do you do in your daily life to be eco-friendly?
- b What are the difficulties for you in being totally eco-friendly?

5 **In your groups, summarise the points you've discussed in Exercise 4. Compare your ideas with the ideas of other groups.**

How eco-aware are you?

1 How many eco-friendly products have you got?

- a none
- b one
- c more than one

2 You should spend a maximum of two minutes in the shower, to save water. Do you agree?

- a It's all very well saying that, but it's just not enough time.
- b It depends – sometimes but not always.
- c It makes sense, because two minutes is more than enough.

3 What is geothermal energy?

- a Sorry, I've never heard of it.
- b I think it's something to do with heating water, but I'm not sure what.
- c It's energy produced from hot underground rocks.

4 In energy terms, what makes a car 'green'?

- a Its size – it's a very small car for just two people.
- b I think it's something to do with the way you drive it. If you drive carefully, you use less fuel, so that makes it green.
- c It doesn't produce much CO_2 because it's powered wholly or partly by electricity instead of petrol or diesel.

5 Which of these applies to you?

- a I don't always remember to switch the lights off when I leave a room.
- b I usually put my laptop into sleep mode when I'm not using it.
- c I switch things off when I'm not using them because I don't want to waste electricity.

6 Is your home energy-efficient?

- a I haven't got a clue, I'm afraid. I've never thought about it.
- b Yes, I think it's quite energy-efficient, but the power isn't from renewable sources.
- c Most of the power is supplied by solar cells and we're careful not to waste electricity.

Analysis

Mostly **a**: You're not very eco-aware, are you?
Mostly **b**: You're quite eco-aware but there's room for improvement.
Mostly **c**: You clearly care about the environment and the future of the planet. Well done!

5.4 Water for life

In this lesson you will...

- understand and use detailed information about water
- use connectives: *while / whereas, although, in order to, so that.*

- **How do we use water in our daily life?**

Listening

35 **1 Listen to the radio programme. What's it about?**

Vocabulary

agriculture	drought	irrigation	washing machines
desalination plants	fresh water	rainfall	wells
drinking water	glaciers	sea water	

35 **2 Work in pairs. The presenters made some notes for the programme. Listen again and complete them using the words from the box.**

- Water covers more than 70% of the Earth's surface.
- Sources: oceans, rivers, lakes, *glaciers*[1], springs and.............[2].
- About 60% of the adult human body is made up of water.
- Essential for human life, for animals and for plants.
- As the world's population increases, more water is needed.
- Daily life: showers, ...[3], dishwashers.
- Average person uses around 150 litres of water a day; great-grandparents used less than 25 litres a day. We use six times more.
- As well as in our homes, water is used in industry and ....[4].
- Clothing industry: 20,000 litres of water for one kilo of cotton (a T-shirt and a pair of jeans).
- Agriculture: 70% of the world's ....[5] supply used for ....[6] (although the percentage does vary from country to country).
- High-income countries use a lot of water; low-income countries use far less.
- Some countries have plenty of water due to high levels of ....[7]; other countries don't have enough water, due to little or no rainfall and this leads to ....[8].
- Where water is scarce, governments are building ....[9] so that ....[10] can be made into ....[11].

3 **Work in groups. Answer these questions.**

- **a** Look at the notes you completed for Exercise 2. Which of the facts do you find the most surprising? Compare your answers around the class.
- **b** What are the presenters' opinions? Do you agree with them?

Use of English Connectives

Connectives join clauses in a sentence. The following connectives show **contrast**:

The average person in our country uses around 150 litres of water a day, ***whereas*** *our great-grandparents used less than 25 litres a day.*

High-income countries use a lot of water, ***while*** *low-income countries use far less.*

And we all still waste water, ***although*** *people are beginning to realise that we must use water carefully for life to continue on Earth.*

Note that *whereas* and *while* have the same meaning.

The connectives *in order to* and *so that* show **purpose**.

We need water ***in order to*** *survive.*

Governments are building desalination plants ***so that*** *sea water can be made into drinking water.*

4 **Use *while / whereas, although, in order to* or *so that* to join these pairs of sentences.**

- **a** Water is a global issue. Individuals can make a difference.
  Water is a global issue, although individuals can make a difference.
- **b** Sun and wind are infinite sources of energy. Water is a finite resource.
- **c** They're building a new reservoir. It's to provide water for towns in the surrounding area.
- **d** When you have a shower, stand in a bowl. You can collect the water and reuse it to water your plants.
- **e** Washing machines use a lot of water. You can select an eco-programme that uses much less.

Speaking

5 **Work in small groups. Use the notes you completed in Exercise 2 to make your own radio or TV programme about water. Try to use some of the connectives in the Use of English box. You can record or video your programme.**

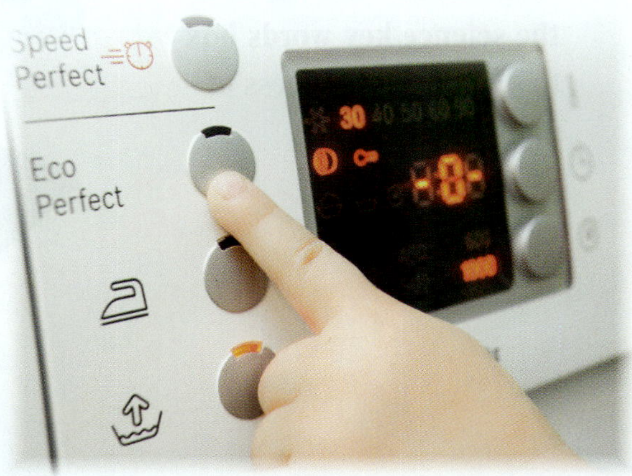

5.5 The lungs of the Earth

In this lesson you will...

- read and understand texts about tropical rainforests and photosynthesis
- discuss the importance of rainforests.

Key words: Science

carbon dioxide
glucose
oxygen
photosynthesis
sunlight
waste product

- **Where do you find tropical rainforests?**

Reading

1 **Read the text on the opposite page. What is the connection between tropical rainforests and biodiversity?**

2 **Find examples in the text of how, in nature, one thing depends on another. Can you think of any other examples?**

3 **Complete these sentences with the correct prepositions. Then look at the explanation of photosynthesis to check your answers.**

a Plants take .... carbon dioxide.
b They take .... water from the ground.
c They take energy .... sunlight.
d Carbon dioxide and water are converted .... glucose and oxygen.
e Plants release oxygen .... the air.

Speaking

4 **Work in pairs. Use the diagram and the words in the science key words box to explain the process of photosynthesis.**

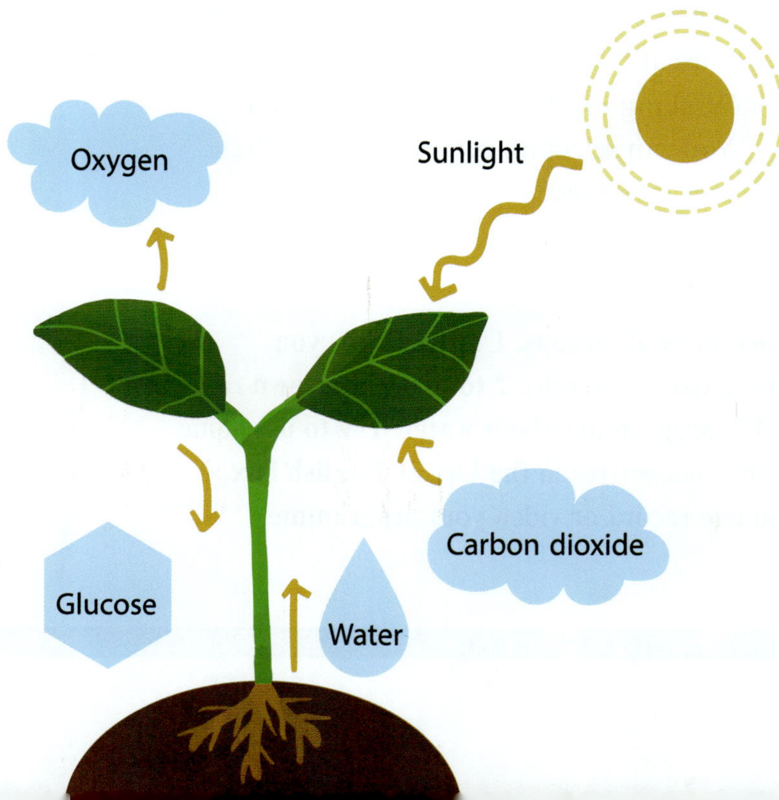

5 Work in small groups. Discuss these questions.

a Why are rainforests called 'the lungs of the Earth'?

b Half of the world's rainforests have disappeared in the last hundred years. If we continue to destroy them at the same rate, they will disappear by the end of this century. How do you feel about this?

Tropical rainforests

Tropical rainforests are home to over 30 million types of plants and animals. That's half of the Earth's wildlife and two-thirds of its plants. The plants provide food and shelter for the many animals that need the rainforest in order to survive.

More than a quarter of our modern medicines come from tropical rainforest plants. For example, the anti-malaria drug quinine is taken from a tree in the Amazon. And there are many more medicines yet to be discovered. Of course, a lot of the things we eat and drink every day come from the rainforest too: nuts, bananas, spices, coffee and chocolate.

Rainforests also help to control our climate. It is thought that the Amazon forest alone holds more than half the Earth's rainwater. The trees take up water from the ground and release it into the atmosphere, where it becomes mist and clouds.

We also depend on trees to keep the air clean. Trees take in the carbon dioxide that we produce and give out the oxygen we need to breathe. This is part of the process of **photosynthesis**.

Rainforests illustrate how important biodiversity is. They show how plants and animals, including human beings, depend on each other in order to survive.

Photosynthesis

Plants can make their own food by the process of photosynthesis. They take in carbon dioxide from the air through their leaves. They take up water from the ground through their roots and they take energy from the sunlight.

carbon dioxide + water ⟶ glucose + oxygen

The energy from sunlight is needed for photosynthesis to take place. In the process of photosynthesis, carbon dioxide and water are converted into oxygen and glucose. Oxygen is a waste product for the plant so the plant releases it into the air. The plant uses glucose as a source of energy for itself.

5.6 Looking back, looking forward

In this lesson you will...

- listen to a debate, identify opinions and recognise an inconsistency in an argument
- role-play a debate about the environment.

Language tip

Identifying inconsistencies

Sometimes people say one thing and then say something else that doesn't agree with what they said first. For example:

I always cycle to the shops. I only take the car if it's raining.

If this person **always** cycles to the shops, that means they never take the car. So how can they only take the car if it's raining? This is an inconsistency.

- **Which environmental issues are in the news at the moment?**

Listening

1 **Listen to a debate about the environment. What are Jessica and Khaled concerned about?**

2 **Listen again. Then answer the questions.**

a What was Jessica horrified about?

b According to Sonia, what is one of the reasons for deforestation?

c How do you think Jessica feels about the answers that Sonia and Sir Michael give?

d How does Rafael argue that protecting the environment is not necessarily a question of money?

e What has recently happened near the school? And what has been the effect?

f What's Rafael's opinion about renewable energy sources?

g Do you think the two politicians have similar opinions about the environment and what should be done?

3 **There is an inconsistency in what Sir Michael says in the debate you've just heard. It's about money and deforestation. What is the inconsistency?**

Use of English Past modals

Use *should have / shouldn't have* + past participle to express criticism and regret.

*We **should have done** something to stop a climate disaster happening.* (I'm criticising people for not doing anything.)

*We **should have acted** earlier.* (I regret that we didn't act earlier.)

Note that *ought to have done* means the same as *should have done*.

*They **ought to have done** this years ago* = They should have done this years ago.

4 **Use *should have / shouldn't have* to complete the second sentence in each pair.**

a I didn't know you were free last weekend. You .... (*send*) me a text.
You should have sent me a text.

b It'll take us hours to drive into town. We .... (*take*) the train.

c You could have recycled those bottles. You .... (*not / throw*) them into the rubbish bin.

d I had to pay for a plastic carrier bag at the supermarket.
I .... (*take*) a shopping bag with me.

e It's very cold in here. You .... (*not / leave*) the door open.

f That TV programme about the Amazon was very good.
You .... (*watch*) it.

Speaking

5 **Work in groups. Imagine a radio debate about the environment, like the one in Exercise 1, is taking place in your school. Role-play the debate.**

You'll need: a presenter, two or more students and two or more politicians (note that the politicians should have different views).

Presenter:

Who wants to start?

What's your answer to that?

Students:

… will be completely destroyed if …

Well, yes, but …

We could have … / They could have …

The government should / shouldn't have ...

We ought to / ought not to have …

Politicians:

It's not just a matter of …

These things take time. It's part of the problem.

It's something that affects us all.

One thing we can do is to …

You've got a good point there …

5.7 Improve your writing

In this lesson you will...

- write an informative account about natural resources.

Your school is contributing to an educational website where students from around the world write about their schools. This month, the topic is 'natural resources'.

1 **Work in pairs. Read the account on the next page. Then answer the questions.**

  a What do you learn about Bali?
  b Why does Kade mention bamboo?
  c Is her school eco-friendly? How do you know?
  d What is Kade's attitude to environmental studies?

2 **Look at the numbered style features in the right-hand column. Answer these questions.**

  a Which three features of the landscape are listed in the first paragraph?
  b Where is there an example of a short sentence followed by a long sentence?
  c Which adjectives describe energy from the sun and energy from water?
  d In the second paragraph, which word is used to introduce two examples?
  e In which paragraphs do these connectives occur: *whereas*, *although*, *so that*?

3 **You're going to write an account of how natural resources are used at your school. Write the first draft of your account.**

- Follow the structure of Kade's account.
- Try to use some of the vocabulary Kade uses.

I live in Kerala, in the southwest of India. My school is not far from the coast. It's surrounded by palm trees. This area is known for beautiful beaches, coconut palms and rice fields. Spices such as pepper, cardamom and cinnamon are grown here, as well as ginger, tea and coffee.

4 **Exchange what you've written with a partner and ask for comments.**

- Are some sentences short and some long?
- Does the account include examples (introduced by *like*, *such as* or *for example*) and connectives (*so that*, *although*, etc.)?

5 **Make any corrections and include suggestions made by your partner.**

6 **Write a final draft.**

Say where you live and give a brief description of the landscape.	I live on the Indonesian island of Bali. Most people think of Bali as a tourist destination, whereas for me it is home. It's a tropical island with forests, mountains and beautiful beaches. The main crop grown here is rice.	1 Include lists of three features to give interest and to make your sentences flow.
Write about a natural resource that is important for your school.	My school is made entirely from bamboo. Bamboo is a natural resource here. It grows easily and quickly. It's much more eco-friendly to use bamboo than to use wood, steel, bricks or concrete. The school has clean energy systems like solar power and a micro-hydro generator. All our electricity is generated from solar and hydro power.	2 Vary the length of the sentences. 3 Use topic-specific vocabulary you have learned in this unit. 4 Give examples to add detail.
	We need electricity for lighting and computers, although we don't need it for heating, because the weather is warm all year round.	5 Use connectives such as *whereas / while, although, in order to, so that* to connect ideas in a sentence.
Give your own opinion to conclude your account.	We have lessons in environmental studies as part of our school curriculum. I think it's very important to learn about the environment so that we understand why we need to protect our natural resources. *Kade*	

5.8 Project challenge

Project 1: A presentation about energy

You're going to write a presentation about energy in your country.

1 Look at the pie charts. What do they show? How do the percentages in the list relate to the sections of the pie charts?

2 Work in groups. Find out which sources of energy are used to provide power in your country today. Use the information to produce a pie chart like the first one.

3 Find out about your country's energy targets and draw a pie chart to illustrate them like the second one. Add a title to your pie chart: By [date].

4 Use your pie charts to give a presentation about how energy is generated now and how it will be generated in the future. Try to use connectives such as *although*, *so that*, *in order to*, etc. Try to make connections to what other students have said.

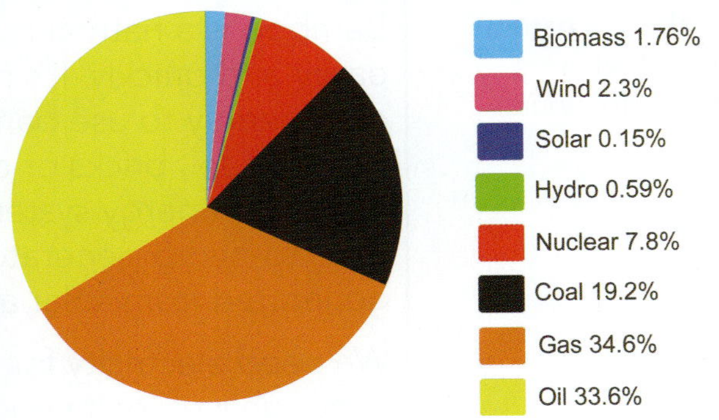

Today

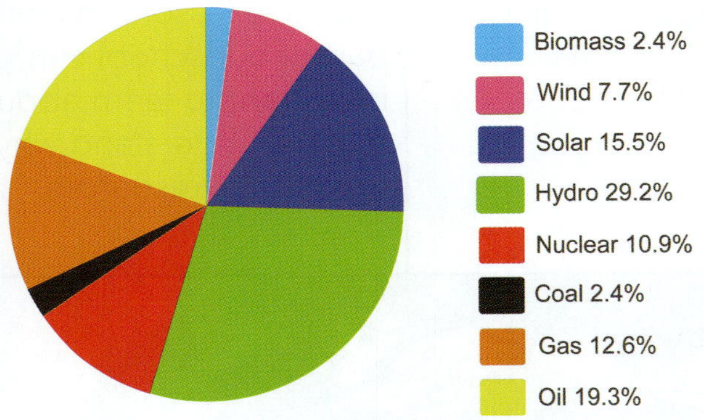

By 2030

As you can see, at the moment, most of our energy is generated from oil and gas, while only a small percentage of our energy is generated from renewable sources.

However, in the future, energy from renewable sources will become much more important in order to meet global targets.

This means that by 2030, 54.8% of our energy will be generated from renewable sources, although oil and gas will continue to be used.

- In your presentation, did you make connections to what other students said?
- Is there anything you would change about your presentation?

Project 2: A poster for an environmental issue campaign

You're going to create a poster for a campaign about an environmental issue.

1 Work in groups. Discuss which environmental issue you think is most important. It can be an issue in your local area, in your city or in your country.

2 How are you going to bring attention to your campaign?

- You're going to start with a poster.
- You need an eye-catching visual image that will attract people's attention. What will you choose?
- You need a slogan. What would work well?

3 Now discuss these possibilities:

- other printed material (school magazine, leaflets)

  We could have an interview in the school magazine, perhaps.

  Yes, but who with?

- traditional media (local radio, local TV)

  What about contacting the local radio station?

  How shall we do that? Shall we send an email?

- social media

  How can we use social media in our campaign?

4 Design the poster and include the slogan.

5 Present your poster to the class and explain your ideas for the campaign.

6 Ask for questions, comments and suggestions from the class.

7 In your group, summarise the feedback you received from the class and make any changes you agree on.

Do you remember that Lila said we should have mentioned climate change?
Yes, and the extreme weather conditions we have had recently.
And Kamal said that we should have thought about contacting the Newsround programme, because it's the sort of thing they're interested in.

- What was the class's reaction to your poster?
- Which of their comments and suggestions did you find useful?

5.9 Speeches

1 Read and listen to these two extracts from Greta Thunberg's book, *No One Is Too Small to Make a Difference*. What tells you that they were written to be spoken rather than to be read?

Extract 1

When I was about eight years old, I first heard about something called climate change, or global warming. Apparently, that was something humans had created by our way of living. I was told to turn off the lights to save energy, and to recycle paper to save resources.

I remember thinking that it was very strange that humans, who are an animal species among others, could be capable of changing the earth's climate.

Because, if we were and if it was really happening, we wouldn't be talking about anything else. As soon as you turned on the TV, everything would be about that. Headlines, radio, newspapers. You would never read or hear about anything else. As if there was a world war going on.

But. No one talked about it. Ever.

If burning fossil fuels was so bad that it threatened our very existence, how could we just continue like before? Why were there no restrictions? Why wasn't it made illegal?

To me, that did not add up. It was too unreal.

2 **apparently:** used to say that you've read or been told something but you're not sure it's true

7 **capable:** able to do something

15 **threaten:** to be likely to harm or destroy something

15 **very:** used to emphasise that you are talking about one particular thing

16 **existence:** the state of being; being alive or real

17 **restrictions:** rules or laws that limit or control what people can do

17 **illegal:** against the law

2 Read the extracts again and answer the questions.

- **a** In Extract 1, what is the issue that Greta Thunberg is concerned about?
- **b** Why do you think she starts by giving the point of view of her eight-year-old self rather than as she is now?
- **c** '…if we were and if it was really happening …' (*line 9*): what is she referring to here?
- **d** She says the media should have reacted 'as if there was a world war going on' (*line 13*). What does she mean by this, and why does she use this simile?
- **e** Why does she use single words as whole sentences (*line 14*)?
- **f** At the end of Extract 1, Greta says '… that did not add up.' What does she mean?

Extract 2

Some people say that we are not doing enough to fight climate change. But that is not true. Because to 'not do enough' you have to do something. And the truth is we are basically not doing anything.

Yes, some people are doing more than they can, but they are too few or too far away from power to make a difference today.

Some people say that the climate crisis is something that we all have created. But that is just another convenient lie. Because if everyone is guilty then no one is to blame.

And someone is to blame. Some people – some companies and some decision-makers in particular – have known exactly what priceless values they are sacrificing to continue making unimaginable amounts of money.

I want to challenge those companies and those decision-makers into real and bold climate action. To set their economic goals aside and to safeguard the future living conditions for humankind. I don't believe for one second that you will rise to that challenge. But I want to ask you all the same.

I ask you to prove me wrong. For the sake of your children, for the sake of your grandchildren. For the sake of life and this beautiful living planet.

I ask you to stand on the right side of history. I ask you to pledge to do everything in your power to push your own business or government in line with a 1.5 °C world.

Will you pledge to do that? Will you pledge to join me, and the people all around the world, in doing whatever it takes?

[22] **basically:** used to say that you are talking about the most important aspects of something

[27] **no one is to blame:** (= no one is to be blamed) no one is responsible for something bad happening

[30] **priceless:** so valuable that you can't say how much it would cost

[30] **sacrifice:** to give up something that is valuable to you in order to help another person

[31] **unimaginable:** that you can't imagine

[32] **challenge:** to ask someone to do something difficult

[33] **bold:** not frightened of difficulty or danger

[34] **set aside:** to put to one side, to forget about temporarily

[34] **safeguard:** to protect from harm or danger

[35] **humankind:** all human beings

[37] **prove someone wrong:** to use evidence to show that someone is wrong

[37] **for the sake of:** in order to help someone or improve their lives

[41] **pledge:** to make a serious promise

g In the first paragraph of Extract 2, how does Greta Thunberg use logic to challenge her audience?

h People most often talk about 'a convenient excuse'. Why does Greta Thunberg talk about a 'convenient lie' (line 26)?

i 'If everyone is guilty, then no one is to blame' (line 27): What is the logic of this?

j Who do you think she means by 'the decision-makers' (line 29)?

k What surprises you most in the paragraph beginning 'I want to challenge ...'?

l Why do you think she mentions people's children and grandchildren here (lines 37–38)?

m What do you notice about the last paragraph?

38

3 **Read and listen to the third extract from *No One Is Too Small to Make a Difference*. Do you think it comes from the beginning or the end of a speech?**

Extract 3

We must change almost everything in our current societies.

The bigger your carbon footprint – the bigger your moral duty.
The bigger your platform – the bigger your responsibility.
Adults keep saying: 'We owe it to the young people to give them hope.'
But I don't want your hope.
I don't want you to be hopeful.
I want you to panic.
I want you to feel the fear I feel every day.
And then I want you to act.
I want you to act as you would in a crisis.
I want you to act as if our house is on fire.
Because it is.

4 **Answer these questions.**

- **a** Why do you think Greta Thunberg doesn't want adults to be hopeful?
- **b** Why does she compare the climate crisis with a house on fire?
- **c** What stylistic features do you notice in this extract?

5 **Work in groups. Practise reading the extract aloud as if you were giving a speech.**

6 **Values Write your own short speech about an environmental issue that concerns you. It could be the issue you chose for Project 2.**

Check your progress

General knowledge quiz

How much do you remember about what you've learned?

1 The guanacaste tree is the national tree of which country in Central America?

2 Name two fossil fuels.

3 Give two examples of renewable energy sources.

4 The main source of nuclear energy is a radioactive substance called u _ _ _ _ _ _ .

5 The chemical symbol for oxygen is O_2. What is the chemical symbol for carbon dioxide?

6 It makes up about 60% of the adult human body. What is it?

7 Choose the correct option: Water covers more than *70% / 80% / 90%* of the Earth's surface.

8 The drug quinine is taken from the bark of the cinchona tree, which is found in the Amazon rainforest. Which disease is it used to treat?

9 Using sunlight, a plant converts carbon dioxide and water into oxygen and a type of sugar that the plant uses for energy. What is this sugar called?

10 What is 'deforestation'?

Vocabulary

1 **Complete the following with the words from the box.**

carbon	electric	energy
friendly	neutral	

a renewable .... sources
b a carbon-............... country
c zero .... emissions
d eco-............... policies
e hydro-............... power stations

2 **Write the words under the correct headings.**

fossil fuels **renewable energy** **radioactive substances**

coal	geothermal	oil	plutonium
solar	uranium	wind	

3 **Match the words with the definitions.**

1 agriculture
2 biodiversity
3 deforestation
4 drought
5 industry
6 irrigation

a a long period when there is no rain
b companies and businesses that produce things to sell
c cutting down trees in a large area, leading to the destruction of forests
d farming
e supplying plants with water so that they will grow
f the variety of plant and animal life

Use of English

1 **A word is missing in each of the following sentences. Rewrite them, putting in the correct word.**

- a Two my cousins live in Australia.
- b Have you seen any the *Life on Earth* programmes on TV?
- c It's one of best TV programmes I have seen.
- d Every one the trees must be saved.
- e We've had a lot rain this month.

2 **Complete these sentences about life in the future using the future passive.**

- a Most of the jobs in the home / do / by robots
  Most of the jobs in the home will be done by robots.
- b Fossil fuels / not / use / in factories
- c Energy / produce / from renewable sources
- d Forests / replant
- e Petrol and diesel cars / replace / by electric cars

3 **Complete the sentences with *although, while / whereas, in order to, so that*.**

- a We often work in groups, ***so that*** we can share ideas.
- b We're going to have a car-free zone outside our school .... improve the air quality.
- c There's only one desalination plant at the moment, ... there are plans for several more.
- d My brother isn't good at languages, ... my sister speaks several languages fluently.

4 **Use *should have / shouldn't have* to write the second sentence.**

- a I feel so tired this morning. (*I / stay up so late*)
  I shouldn't have stayed up so late.
- b I got into trouble for being late for school. (*I / get up earlier*)
- c I can't answer any of the questions in this test. (*I / do more revision*)
- d The holiday was meant to be a surprise and now everybody knows, thanks to you! (*you / tell everybody*)

Summary checklist

I can

- ☐ describe different ways in which energy is generated.
- ☐ discuss the advantages and disadvantages of a variety of energy sources.
- ☐ summarise ideas from a discussion.
- ☐ understand the importance of tropical rainforests and describe the process of photosynthesis.
- ☐ give a presentation about energy in my country, now and in the future.

6 Natural wonders

In this unit you will...

- **ask** and **answer** questions in a quiz about geographical features
- **understand** a scientific explanation
- **listen** to and **have** a conversation about a natural wonder
- **listen** to and **take part** in a quiz about wildlife
- **find out** what makes the sky blue
- **use** a radio phone-in programme as a model for a role-play
- **write** an account of a place in your country that could be a World Heritage Site
- **give** a presentation of a natural wonder of the world
- **read** an extract from a novel about a Māori family in New Zealand
- **write** a scene to continue a story.

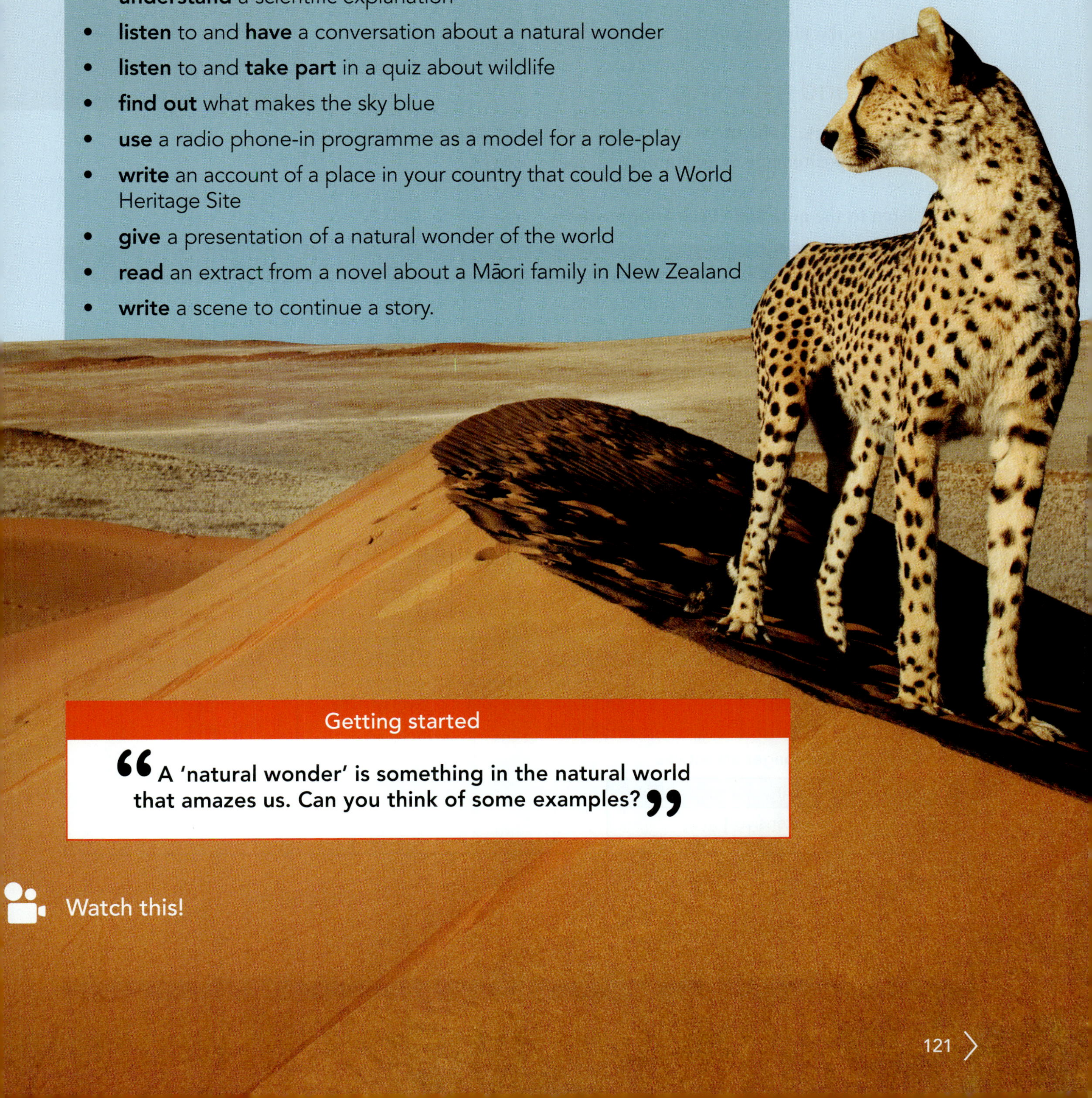

Getting started

“A ‘natural wonder’ is something in the natural world that amazes us. Can you think of some examples?”

Watch this!

6.1 Highest, longest, deepest

In this lesson you will...

- ask and answer questions in a quiz about geographical features
- use comparative and superlative adjectives.

- **Where is the highest point in your country?**

Reading and listening

1 **Work in pairs. Take turns to ask and answer the questions in the quiz on the opposite page. Make a note of your answers.**

39 **2** **Listen to the quiz and check your answers.**

Use of English Comparatives and superlatives of adjectives

Complete the tables with words from the quiz.

One-syllable adjectives

Adjective	Comparative	Superlative	Notes
high	higher	the	Most adjectives: add *-er*, *-est*
large	larger	the largest	Adjectives ending in *-e*: add *-r*, *-st*
thin	thinner	the thinnest	Adjectives with one vowel followed by one consonant: double the consonant

Irregular comparatives and superlatives

Adjective	Comparative	Superlative
good	better	the best
bad	worse	the worst

Two-syllable adjectives

Adjective	Comparative	Superlative	Notes
narrow	narrower	....	Check in a dictionary for comparative and superlative forms of two-syllable adjectives.
active	more active	....	

Three-syllable and longer adjectives

Adjective	Comparative	Superlative
extensive	more extensive	....

Remember, to compare two things that are or aren't equal, use *(not) as … as*.

*Norway is**n't as** narrow **as** Chile.*

You can use *far* and *much* before a comparative for emphasis.

*The Amazon is **far / much** more extensive than any other rainforest.*

1 Which is the highest mountain on Earth?

- A K2
- B Mount Everest
- C Annapurna

2 Which is the longest river in the world?

- A The Yangtze
- B The Nile
- C The Rio Grande

3 The deepest part of the ocean is called the Mariana Trench. Where is it?

- A It's in the Indian Ocean.
- B It's in the Atlantic Ocean.
- C It's in the Pacific Ocean.

4 What is the longest and narrowest country in the world?

- A Norway in Scandinavia
- B Chile in South America
- C Somalia on the east coast of Africa

5 Which is the most active volcano in the world?

- A Mount Etna in Italy
- B Kilauea in Hawaii
- C Popocatépetl in Mexico

6 Which is the most extensive rainforest on the planet?

- A The Congo rainforest in Africa.
- B The South-East Asian rainforest.
- C The Amazon in South America.

Vocabulary

Use *the* with:

- groups of mountains and islands: the Himalayas, the Philippines
- rivers, seas and oceans: the Ganges, the Mediterranean, the Arctic Ocean
- most geographical regions: the East, the Punjab
- deserts: the Sahara

Don't use *the* with:

- continents, most countries and groups of countries: Africa, China, South America
- lakes, individual islands, and most mountains: Lake Titicaca, Sicily, Mont Blanc

3 **Find examples in the quiz in Exercise 1 to add to the examples above.**

Speaking and writing

4 **Work in pairs. You're going to write two more multiple-choice questions for the quiz using comparative and superlative adjectives.**

- First discuss ideas for the questions. Make sure you know the answers.
- Write your questions. Look at the rules for using *the* with geographical names.
- Ask other members of the class to answer your questions.
- You can listen to a model conversation to help you.

What's the biggest lake in Turkey? Is it Lake Tuz, Lake Eber or Lake Van?

6.2 Light at night

In this lesson you will...

- understand a scientific explanation
- identify an inconsistency in a text.

Key words: Science

chemical reaction
compound
enzyme
organism
process
to be exposed to
to emit

- **What kinds of light do you see in the natural world?**

Reading

1 **Read the extracts on the opposite page. Where might you find them?**

2 **Work in pairs. Student A reads the text about Puerto Rico. Student B reads the text about bioluminescence.**

Student B asks Student A these questions:

- Why does the writer recommend going to Mosquito Bay?
- Where is Mosquito Bay and what's it like?
- Should I go during the day or at night? Why?
- What does bioluminescence look like?

Student A asks Student B these questions:

- If an animal is bioluminescent, what can it do?
- What kind of animals are bioluminescent?
- What about plants?
- What substance do plants and animals have that makes them bioluminescent?

3 **There's an inconsistency in the text about what you can do at Puerto Rico's bioluminescent bays. What is it?**

Remember

Remember that an inconsistency is when someone says or writes something and then says or writes something else that doesn't agree with it.

Writing

4 **Find out more. Work in pairs to find the information to answer this question. Try to include some of the words in the science key words box.**

A firefly is a bioluminescent insect. Explain the process that makes it bioluminescent.

What to do in PUERTO RICO

The most amazing thing you'll ever see: bioluminescence

plankton – very small plants and animals that live in the sea and are eaten by fish

Puerto Rico has three of the most spectacular bioluminescent bays in the world. They are Laguna Grande in Fajardo, La Parguera in Lajas and Mosquito Bay in Vieques. The brightest and most magical of them all is Mosquito Bay. La Parguera is not as impressive as Mosquito Bay, but it's the only one of the three bays in which you are allowed to swim.

Mosquito Bay is on the small island of Vieques, just off the east coast of Puerto Rico. It's a sheltered bay where you'll find a special kind of plankton that emits a bright blue-green light. One of the best ways to experience bioluminescence is in a glass-bottomed kayak. The movement of the kayak causes waves, which make the plankton glow. The best time to see this is at night, ideally when there is very little moonlight, because then the luminescence is more visible. It's the most magical experience. It's like floating in a sea of stars!

If you don't like the idea of kayaking, you can go on a guided boat tour of Mosquito Bay at night. You'll be able to swim and see the water coming off your hands like sparks of light.

You can get to Vieques by plane from San Juan or you can take the ferry from Fajardo or Ceiba.

What is bioluminescence?

Although humans can't create their own light, some animals can, in a process called bioluminescence. Fireflies are perhaps the best-known example, although many other species are bioluminescent, including glow-worms, anglerfish and octopuses. Even some plants, such as mushrooms and other fungi, are bioluminescent.

What allows some plants and animals to create their own light? It's all about energy. Most people know that chemical energy can be released as heat. That's how the food we eat gets transformed into body heat. In bioluminescent organisms, that chemical energy can also be released in the form of light.

Bioluminescent organisms can glow in complete darkness. They contain a unique compound called luciferin. When luciferin is exposed to oxygen, a chemical reaction, aided by an enzyme called luciferase, emits light.

6.3 Look at this!

In this lesson you will...

- listen to and have a conversation about a natural wonder
- use demonstrative, indefinite and quantitative pronouns.

- **Are there any mountains, volcanoes or rocky areas in your country? Where are they?**

Listening

41 **1** **Look at the picture. What does it show? Listen to the conversation to find out.**

2 **Complete the sentences. Then listen again and check.**

a The boy thinks the picture looks like a scene from a ....

b The mushroom-shaped towers are .... formations.

c The ash from a .... eruption became soft rock.

d Over time, the rock was eroded by wind and ....

e Some of the towers are about .... metres high.

f People carved out the .... of the rock to make places to live.

g They made .... towns where they could hide from their enemies.

h Today, some are .... where you can stay.

Cappadocia, Turkey

Use of English Pronouns

A pronoun is a word that is used instead of a noun.

Look at ***this****. = Look at* *the picture*.

What are ***those****? = What are* *the things in the picture*?

Demonstrative pronouns	Indefinite pronouns	Quantitative pronouns
this, that (singular) *these, those* (plural)	For example: *somebody, something, anybody, anything, nobody, nothing*	For example: *some, any, all, both, either, much, many, more, most, enough, several, a little, a few, another, none*

Note that the pronoun *one* has a plural form:

Look at the ***one*** *in the picture.*

Are these the only ***ones****?*

Use *a / an* if there is an adjective before *one*:

There's ***one*** *in the picture.*

There's ***an old one*** *in the picture.*

3 Use pronouns from the Use of English box to complete this conversation.

A: Are there any mountains in Oman?

B: Yes, there are .... Look, here's a picture of ....

A: Wow! What's it called?

B: It's called Jebel Shams. It's the highest mountain in Oman.

A: Are there any towns or villages in the area?

B: Yes, there are a .... There's .... in the picture. It's quite a new .... , but there are some very old .... where .... lives any more.

Speaking

4 Work in pairs. Each student finds a photo of a mountain, a lake, a rock formation or other natural feature. Have a conversation about it, like the ones in Exercises 1 and 3.

Jebel Shams, in Oman

6.4 Fastest, longest, furthest

In this lesson you will...

- listen to and take part in a quiz about wildlife
- use comparative and superlative adverbs.

- **Which animals live a long time? Which animals can run very fast? Which birds fly long distances?**

A hummingbird

Listening and vocabulary

42

1 Listen. Note down the correct answer for each question.

a Of these three animals, which one runs the fastest?
Is it a **leopard**, an **antelope** or a **cheetah**?

b Which animal lives the longest?
Is it a **killer whale**, an **elephant** or a **giant tortoise**?

c Which animal's heart beats the most quickly?
Is it a **hummingbird**, a **mouse** or a **cat**?

d Which animal remembers faces and places best?
Is it a **shark**, a **swan** or an **elephant**?

e Which animal recognises its own species through sound most easily?
Is it a **wolf**, an **owl** or a **dolphin**?

f Which animal sleeps the longest each day?
Is it an **owl**, a **cat** or a **koala**?

Use of English Comparatives and superlatives of adverbs

Most comparative and superlative adverbs are made with *more* and *most*.

Adverb	Comparative adverb	Superlative adverb
slowly	more slowly	(the) most slowly

Short adverbs usually have comparative forms ending in ***-er***.

early	earlier	the earliest
fast	faster	the fastest
hard	harder	the hardest
high	higher	the highest
late	later	the latest
long	longer	the longest
low	lower	the lowest
near	nearer	the nearest
soon	sooner	the soonest

Irregular adverbs

well	better	the best
badly	worse	the worst
far	further/farther	the furthest/farthest
much	more	the most
little	less	the least

42

2 **Write two sentences for each correct answer in Exercise 1. Listen again if you need to.**

A cheetah runs the fastest. It runs faster than an antelope or a leopard.

> **Use of English   Comparative adverb structures**
>
> You can use these words to be more specific about comparative adverbs: *far, much, a lot, quite a lot, a bit / slightly*
>
> *A cheetah can run* ***far faster*** *than a leopard.* (cheetah up to 120 km/h, leopard up to 56 km/h)
>
> *An antelope can run* ***slightly faster*** *than a lion.* (antelope up to 89 km/h, lion up to 80 km/h)

3 **Write two or three sentences for each set of prompts.**

a **beats:** a camel's heart 30 bpm, a horse's heart 40 bpm, a mouse's heart 600 bpm
A horse's heart beats quite a lot faster than a camel's heart.
A mouse's heart beats far faster. A mouse's heart beats the fastest of all three.

b **lives:** A killer whale 35 years, an elephant 56 years, a giant tortoise 150 years

c **swims:** A penguin 35 km/h, a blue shark 69 km/h, a blue fin tuna 74 km/h

d **flies:** An Arctic tern up to 100,000 km/year, a swallow up to 19,000 km/year, a peregrine falcon up to 25,000 km/year

Speaking

4 **Work in pairs. Talk about what you've learned from this lesson and what you found interesting.**

An antelope

6.5 Just look at the sky!

In this lesson you will...

- find out about what makes the sky blue
- give a scientific explanation of the colour of the sky.

Key words: Physics

atmosphere
frequency
molecule

- **A survey of ten countries across four continents showed that blue is the world's favourite colour. Why do you think this is?**

Reading

1 **Why is the sky blue? If you don't know the answer, try to think of a possible explanation.**

2 **Read the following explanation. Did anyone in the class get the answer right, or come close to the correct answer?**

Question

Why is the sky blue?

Answer

Light arriving from the Sun hits the molecules in the air and is scattered in all directions. The amount of scattering depends (dramatically) on the frequency – that is, the colour of the light. Blue light, which has a high frequency, is scattered ten times more than red light, which has a lower frequency, so the 'background' scattered light we see is blue.

This same process also explains the beautiful red colours at sunset. When the Sun is low on the horizon, its light has to pass through a large amount of atmosphere on its way to us. During the trip, blue light is scattered away, but red light, which is less susceptible to scattering, can continue on its direct path to our eyes.

Vocabulary

3 Match these words with their definitions.

a	molecule	1	the gases around the Earth
b	scatter	2	the line where the sky and the land or sea seem to meet
c	frequency	3	likely to be affected by something
d	horizon	4	the smallest unit of a substance, with two or more atoms
e	atmosphere	5	to move quickly in different directions
f	susceptible	6	the number of times that a light wave (or a sound wave or a radio wave) vibrates (moves up and down)

Writing and speaking

4 Work in groups. You're going to give a presentation about the colour of the sky. Below, there are some slides you can use. Plan your presentation, using the slides and the information in Exercise 2.

5 Each group gives a presentation. Other groups listen and ask questions about the presentation to make sure they understand.

What are molecules?

I don't understand 'frequency'. What does it mean?

Light is made up of all the colours of the rainbow: red, orange, yellow, green, blue, indigo, violet.

Light travels in waves. Blue waves are shorter than red waves.

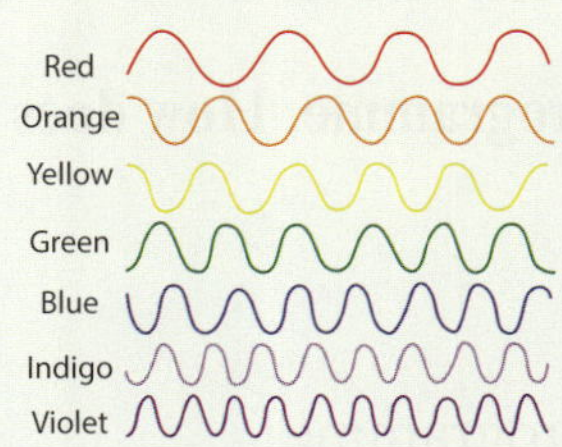

In the air, there are molecules of nitrogen, oxygen and other gases.

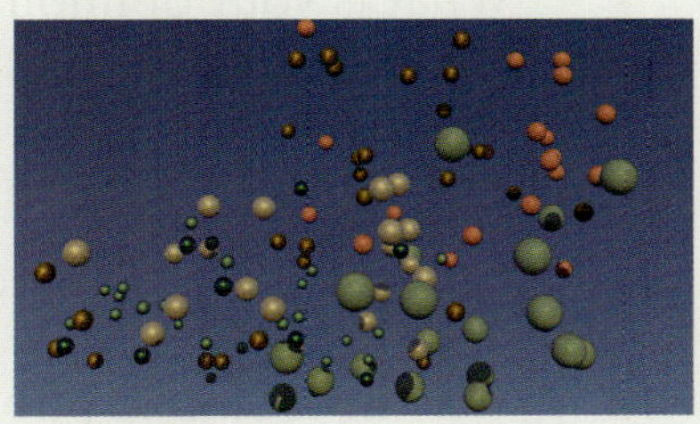

6.6 Use your human superpowers

In this lesson you will...

- use a radio phone-in programme as a model for a role-play
- learn and use multi-word verbs.

- **Are radio phone-in programmes a good idea? Why? / Why not?**

Listening

43 **1** **Listen to the first part of a radio programme called 'It's up to you'. What sort of programme is it?**

2 **Listen again and answer these questions.**

- a Why does Suresh phone the programme?
- b Suresh's teacher tells him off for 'daydreaming'. What is 'daydreaming'?
- c Vanessa says that 'not all habits are good habits'. How does this relate to what Suresh says?
- d Vanessa says that going to bed earlier can have a 'knock-on effect'. What does this mean, and what examples does she give?
- e What advice does Vanessa give Suresh?
- f What is your opinion of Vanessa's advice?

44 **3** **Now listen to the next part of the programme. How does Vanessa make Jamila feel at ease?**

4 **Answer the questions.**

- a Why does Jamila phone the programme?
- b Vanessa gives an example of a fear that a lot of people have. What is it?
- c Why is this fear not 'rational'?
- d Vanessa tells Jamila, 'You just need to take a step back.' What does she mean?
- e Vanessa mentions one way in which she is similar to Jamila. What is it?
- f How does Vanessa encourage Jamila to ask her sports teacher about playing tennis?

5 **Read each pair of sentences. Complete the second sentence of each pair so that it means the same as the first. (They are all in the radio programme you have just heard.)**

a I'm in trouble quite a lot.
I get .... trouble quite a lot.

b I'm not doing well at school
I'm not getting .... well at school.

c I find it hard to be as good as the other students in maths.
I can't keep .... the other students in maths.

d I can't just approach the teacher and say I'd like to try.
I can't just go .... the teacher and say I'd like to try.

e Say that you need a bit of encouragement.
Say that you could do .... a bit of encouragement.

f The teachers get annoyed with me for not paying attention.
The teachers tell me .... for not paying attention.

g You need sleep.
You can't do .... sleep.

h Your brain gradually starts thinking that it's normal to go to bed late.
Your brain gets .... the habit of thinking that it's normal to go to bed late.

Use of English
Multi-word verbs (phrasal and prepositional verbs)

Multi-word verbs are verbs made up of two or more words – a verb like *get* followed by a preposition or adverbial particle: *to* ***get into*** *trouble, to* ***get on*** *well.*

There can be more than one preposition/ adverbial particle after a verb. For example, *Suresh's teacher wants him to* ***get on with*** *his work, rather than daydreaming.*

Speaking

6 **Work in pairs. Act out either the first phone call to the programme (from Suresh) or the second (from Jamila). Practise using the multi-word verbs in Exercise 5.**

Try to include some of the following phrases:

I suppose so.	**I'm sure that ...**	**Is that right?**
No, not really.	**You never know, ...**	**No, not at all.**
The problem is ...	**For example, ...**	**Exactly.**
You'll find that ...	**It doesn't make sense.**	
It has a knock-on effect.	**Me too!**	

7 **Work in groups. Role-play the following situation.**

The next caller to the programme is having problems because he / she is new at school, is quite shy and doesn't have any friends. You can have several experts and one caller.

6.7 Improve your writing

In this lesson you will...

- write an account of a place in your country that could be a World Heritage Site.

UNESCO, the United Nations Educational, Scientific and Cultural Organization, identifies **World Heritage Sites** with the aim of protecting and preserving them. They can be geographical areas, such as the Canadian Rocky Mountains; they can be places where animals need protection, like the Serengeti National Park in Tanzania; and they can be buildings, such as the Taj Mahal in India.

1 **Work with a partner. Read the account written by Lena. Choose two or three phrases that show that she is very enthusiastic about this place.**

2 **Notice how Lena structures her account:**

- Paragraph 1 Introduction
- Paragraph 2 Getting there
- Paragraph 3 Things to do when you are there
- Paragraph 4 The reason for choosing this place

Put each of the following under the correct paragraph heading.

a She compares this place with other beautiful areas in the world.
b She explains where the lakes are in relation to a town in the area.
c She gives examples of what you might see in the surrounding countryside.
d She gives information about a town to go to when you first get there.
e She gives information about two ways you can see the area.
f She introduces herself.
g She introduces the place she's going to talk about.
h She says how big it is.
i She talks about who goes there.

Paragraph 1 Introduction

f She introduces herself.

Language tip

Lena mentions *deer*, *moose* and *boar* in her account. Notice that these are plural nouns (like *sheep* and *fish*).

Hello! My name is Lena. I live in a village in the north-east of Poland, in an area called Masuria. In Polish, we call it the 'land of a thousand lakes', and it is so special that I think it should be a World Heritage Site. It's one of the most popular tourist destinations for Polish people and visitors from nearby European countries, but it's not well known outside Europe. It covers an area of 52,000 km^2.

You can get to the Masurian Lake District by train, bus or car. The best place to stay when you arrive is Olsztyn (pronounced 'Olshtin'). It's a very attractive city, the biggest place in the area and the easiest to get to. The lakes are to the east of Olsztyn. The largest lakes, and the most popular ones, are Lake Śniardwy (109 km^2) and Lake Mamry (104 km^2).

One of the most exciting ways of exploring the lakes is by canoe or kayak. You can even do a 10-day trip through 18 lakes that are connected by small rivers. The banks are covered in thick forests that are home to the most wonderful animals, like moose, deer, boar and even wolves. Canoeing and kayaking are great fun, but if you prefer something a little less energetic, you can spend a day cycling round one of the lakes. You can rent bicycles more easily than canoes.

Other countries have higher mountains, bigger forests and more ancient buildings than Poland. However, the Masurian Lake District was recently chosen as one of the 28 finalists in the 'New 7 Wonders of Nature' competition. That is why I think it should be a World Heritage Site.

3 **Lena uses comparatives and superlatives in her account. How many can you find?**

She says that cycling is a little less energetic than canoeing or kayaking. (comparative: *a little less energetic*)

She says Olsztyn is the best place to stay. (superlative: *the best place*)

4 **Choose a place that you think should be a World Heritage Site. Write a draft account of it for a partner school in another country. Use Lena's account as a model.**

- Write four paragraphs.
- Use your answers to Exercise 2 to order the information you give.
- Try to include some comparatives and superlatives.

5 **Check your account.**

- Have you included all the points that Lena included?
- Have you included some comparatives and superlatives?

6.8 Project challenge

Project 1: A presentation

You're going to give a presentation of a natural wonder of the world.

1 Work in groups. Choose a natural wonder for your presentation. (Each group should choose a different natural wonder.)

2 Your presentation should contain between six and ten slides. Make notes of what each slide should feature. For example:

Slide 1:
Photo 1, Iguaçu Falls, with a caption:
Iguaçu Falls, the largest waterfalls in the world

Slide 2:
Map showing Argentina, Brazil and the Falls.
Labels for the map:
ARGENTINA
BRAZIL
Iguaçu Falls

Slide 3:
Repeat Photo 1.
Add a caption and arrows to show longest drop and width
82 metres
2.7 kilometres

3 Find your photos. If you can't find the ones you want, revise your plan.

4 Write a draft of your script. Try to include some comparatives and superlatives.

Slide 1
These are the Iguaçu Falls, the largest waterfalls in the world.

Slide 2
As you can see, the Iguaçu Falls are on the border of Argentina and Brazil.

5 Check your script. Do the captions on the slides match the script?

6 Rehearse your presentation. Check the pronunciation of difficult words.

7 Give your presentation to the other groups in the class.

8 Ask for comments on your presentation.

- Which of the places that your classmates presented were the most interesting and why?
- What were the best aspects of your group's presentation?

Project 2: Question and answer session

You're going to have a question and answer session comparing two animals.

1 Work in groups. Each group chooses a different pair of animals to compare. For example:

- a tiger and a lion
- a cheetah and a leopard
- an alligator and a crocodile
- an eagle and a hawk
- a tortoise and a turtle.

2 Find out all you can about the differences between the animals, so that you are well prepared to answer questions about them.

3 Make notes on the differences. Here are some ideas:

- size
- weight
- where they live
- how long they live
- what they eat.

4 Have your question and answer session. Here is an example:

A: Which animals have you chosen?
B: Turtles and tortoises.
A: What's the difference between a tortoise and a turtle?
B: Well, a tortoise is in fact a kind of turtle!
A: Oh, I didn't know that!
B: But we usually call the animal that can only live on land a tortoise. Turtles live in water, at least some of the time.
A: Are there any other differences?
B: Yes. Tortoises have shells that are heavier than turtle shells.
A: Anything else?
B: Tortoises have feet that look like very small elephant feet, whereas turtles have webbed feet.
A: That's really interesting. How long do they live?
B: Tortoises live much longer than turtles.
A: How much longer?
B: Galápagos tortoises live for over 150 years. The oldest tortoise alive today is 188 years old. Turtles, on the other hand, live for between 10 and 80 years.

5 Group A reports back to Group B on what they have learned about the animals. Group B checks that all the information is correct.

- What have you learned from doing this project?
- How has this project helped you to improve your English?

6.9 Fiction

Witi Ihimaera is a writer from New Zealand. He was born in the North Island, near the coast. His novel, *The Whale Rider*, features both the Māori culture and the ocean. He has written several novels and also many short stories. *The Whale Rider* was made into a film starring the young actress Keisha Castle-Hughes, who was born in Australia and grew up in New Zealand, as the main character, Kahu.

1 **What do you know about New Zealand and the Māori people?**

2 **Read the summary of the story so far. Then answer the questions.**

a Why does Kahu's great-grandfather set tasks for the boys from the community?

b One of these tasks is mentioned. What is it?

c What does Kahu call her great-grandfather?

d Who are Rawiri and Nani Flowers?

The story so far …

Māoris believe that leadership is hereditary: it passes to the firstborn son and then to his first son. In *The Whale Rider* by Witi Ihimaera, Kahu's great-grandfather is the chief of his community, and he was disappointed when Kahu was born that she wasn't a boy. He looks for possible future leaders among the boys in the community. He teaches them Māori skills and sets them special tasks. In one of these tasks, he takes the boys out on the sea in a boat and throws a special stone into the water. The boys have to dive down, find the stone and bring it back. But none of them can do it. Kahu's great-grandfather is very disappointed and sad about this.

Kahu loves her great-grandfather, who she calls 'Paka', and she wants to make him happy. So the next morning, when Kahu's uncle Rawiri is taking his boat out, she asks if she can go with him. Kahu's great-grandmother, Nani Flowers, goes with them too. She knows the place where the stone was thrown into the water.

45

3 **Read and listen to the extract from Chapter 3. Then answer these questions.**

a Who is telling the story?

b What impression do you get of Kahu and of Nani Flowers?

4 **What do the verbs in each group have in common? Find them in the story and, with a partner, try to work out their meaning. Use a dictionary to help you.**

Group 1	Group 2	Group 3	Group 4
do a duck dive (line 15)	scream (line 8)	jab (line 8)	gasp (line 25)
dog paddle (line 22)	yell (line 12)	push (line 10)	swallow (line 25)
float (line 23)	cry (line 42)	throw (line 13)	cough (line 26)
drown (line 29)		wave (line 21)	splutter (line 27)
drift (line 48)		grab (line 34)	

Kahu said simply, "I'll get it."

Before we could stop her she stood up and dived overboard. Until that moment I had never even known that she could swim.

Nani's mouth made a big 'O'. Then the breath rushed into her lungs and she screamed, "Oh, no!" She jabbed me hard and said, "Go after her, Rawiri, *Go.*" She virtually pushed me over the side of the rowboat.

"Give me the diving mask," I yelled. Nani Flowers threw it at me and quickly I put it on. I took three deep breaths and did a duck dive.

I couldn't see her. The sea looked empty. There was only a small stingray flapping down towards the reef.

Then I got a big fright because the stingray turned around and, smiling, waved at me. It was Kahu in her white dress and sandals, dog paddling down to the sea floor, her braids floating around her head.

I gasped and swallowed sea water. I came to the surface coughing and spluttering.

"Where is she!" Nani Flowers screamed. "Has she drowned? Oh, no, my Kahu." And before I could stop her she jumped in beside me, just about emptying the whole ocean. She didn't even give me a chance to explain as she grabbed the mask off me and put it on. Then she tried to swim underwater, but her dress was so filled with air that no matter how hard she tried she remained on the surface like a balloon with legs kicking out of it. I doubt if she could have gotten deeper anyway because she was so fat she couldn't sink.

"Oh, Kahu," Nani Flowers cried again. But this time I told her to take a deep breath and, when she was looking underwater, to watch where I would point.

We went beneath the surface. Suddenly I pointed down. Kahu was searching the reef, drifting around the coral. Nani Flowers' eyes widened with disbelief.

Whatever it was Kahu was searching for, she was having difficulty finding it. But just then white shapes came speeding out of the dark towards her. I thought they were sharks, and Nani Flowers began to blow bubbles of terror.

They were dolphins. They circled around Kahu and seemed to be talking to her. She nodded and grabbed one around its body. As quick as a flash, the dolphins sped her to another area of the reef and stopped. Kahu seemed to say, "Down here?" and the dolphins made a nodding motion.

5 Work with a partner. Discuss these questions.

a Who is the comic character in this extract?

b Student A: cover the left-hand column of the text (lines 1 to 31). Tell Student B that part of the story.

Student B: cover the right-hand column of the text (lines 32 to 63). Tell Student A that part of the story.

6 Read and listen to the next part of the extract. Then answer the questions.

a What are the two things Kahu finds in the sea?

b What do you learn about Kahu from this story and what do you learn about her family?

Suddenly Kahu made a quick darting gesture. She picked something up, inspected it, appeared satisfied with it, and went back to the dolphins. Slowly the girl and the dolphins rose towards us. But just as they were midway, Kahu stopped again. She kissed the dolphins goodbye and gave Nani Flowers a heart attack by returning to the reef. She picked up a crayfish and resumed her upward journey. The dolphins were like silver dreams as they disappeared.

Nani Flowers and I were treading water when Kahu appeared between us, smoothing her hair back from her face and blinking away the sea water. Nani Flowers, sobbing, hugged her close in the water.

"I'm all right, Nani," Kahu laughed.

She showed the crayfish to us. "This is for Paka's tea," she said. "And you can give him back his stone."

She placed the stone in Nani Flowers' hands.

7 Write the next scene of the book.

- What happened next?
- What do you think Kahu said to her great-grandfather?
- What do you think he said to her?

Try to follow the narrative style of the extract.

Remember to use " " to show what people actually said. Start a new line for each person who speaks.

Keisha Castle-Hughes as Kahu in the film *Whale Rider*

Check your progress

General knowledge quiz

How much do you remember about what you've learned?

1 Which is the longest river in the world?

2 Which is higher, Mount Everest or K2?

3 It's the longest and narrowest country in the world and it's in South America. Which country is it?

4 What is the Mariana Trench and where is it?

5 What is plankton?

6 Which animal can run faster, a leopard or a cheetah?

7 They say this animal never forgets, and it's true that it has a very good memory for faces and places. What is it?

8 What is this bird called and what is special about its heartbeat?

9 Name the colours of the rainbow.

10 Which has the higher frequency, blue light or red light?

Vocabulary

1 **Add *the* where necessary.**

- a We went to .... south of France.
- b Where is .... Lake Erie?
- c Have you skied in .... Alps?
- d I'd like to sail down .... Nile.
- e Look at this photo of .... Atlas Mountains!
- f .... Martinique is an island in the Caribbean.

2 **Read the descriptions and complete the names of the animals.**

- a It belongs to the cat family. It has yellow fur with black spots. It's stronger and heavier than a cheetah. *l* _ _ _ _ _ _
- b It's a bird with large eyes. It hunts small animals at night. People say this bird is very wise. *o* _ _
- c This grey mammal lives in the sea and is a known for its playfulness. *d* _ _ _ _ _ _
- d This large fish has sharp teeth and can be dangerous. *s h* _ _ _

Use of English

1 **Complete the second sentence so that it means the same as the first.**

- a I'm nowhere near as good at geography as you.
  You're ***much better at geography than me***. (*much*)
- b The film is nowhere near as interesting as the book.
  The book .... (*far*)
- c This photo of a tiger is better than all the others.
  .... of all. (*the best*)
- d Asia is the largest continent by far.
  Asia .... (*much*) all the other continents.
- e An eagle has very good eyesight. An elephant does not.
  An elephant's eyesight .... (*much*)

2 Rewrite the conversation, replacing the underlined words with a pronoun from the box.

a few	none	one	these
ones	someone		

A: We need some pictures of animals for our project.

B: What about <u>the pictures in this magazine</u>?

A: Are they the only <u>pictures</u> we've got?

B: There are <u>one or two pictures</u> on the website that we looked at earlier.

A: Oh, yes. But there were <u>no pictures</u> showing animals in the wild.

B: What else do we need?

A: A dictionary, to check our spelling.

B: There's <u>a dictionary</u> over there.

A: And we need <u>a person</u> to design the poster.

B: I'll do it.

A: OK. Let's start!

3 Complete this table.

Adjective	Adverb	Comparative adverb	Superlative adverb
good	well	better	....
bad	badly	....	worst
high	high	higher	....
careful	carefully	....	most carefully
clear	clearly	more clearly	....
quick	quickly	....	....
safe	....	....	....

4 Use a comparative or superlative adverb from Exercise 3 to complete these sentences.

a You can cross the road much ***more safely*** if you use the pedestrian crossing.

b Ella has got two sisters. They all sing really well, but the youngest sister sings the ....

c My younger brother says he could get home far .... if he took his skateboard to school.

d I've skied much .... since I nearly broke my leg!

e You did so well in the high jump. You jumped the .... of anyone in the school!

Summary checklist

I can

- ☐ talk about a natural feature, such as a mountain or a lake.
- ☐ compare animals in terms of speed, memory, life expectancy, etc.
- ☐ understand and give a scientific presentation.
- ☐ write about a place that I think should be a World Heritage Site.
- ☐ give a presentation about a natural wonder of the world.
- ☐ take part in a question and answer session comparing two animals.

7 Historical figures

In this unit you will...

- **listen** to opinions about historical figures
- **read** an account of a historical figure
- **listen** to and **role-play** an interview about the achievements of a leader
- **learn** about and **discuss** famous artists, musicians and writers
- **learn** about the Islamic Golden Age
- **listen** to and **report** a conversation about an unusual exhibition
- **write** a short biography of a historical figure
- **give** a presentation about a historical figure
- **write** an interview with a historical figure
- **read** an extract from a book set in the First World War
- **write** a conversation between characters in a story.

Getting started

"Who do you think are the most interesting historical figures? Why are they remembered?"

Watch this!

7.1 Leaders, rulers and explorers

Mahatma Gandhi

In this lesson you will...

- listen to opinions about historical figures
- use the past continuous.

- **Think of an example of each of the people listed in the box below.**

queen	hero (heroes)	president	emperor	ruler
king	civil rights activist	explorer	empress	

Elizabeth I

Listening

47 **1** **Listen to the interviews with people talking about important historical figures. Which of the names do you recognise? What do you know about them?**

Nelson Mandela

Vocabulary

2 **Find words in the vocabulary box to describe each of the people in the photos.**

Mahatma Gandhi ***a civil rights activist***

Napoleon Bonaparte

Rosa Parks

Ibn Battuta

Speaking tip

Roman numerals are used in the written titles of kings and queens after their name. Notice how you say them.

Elizabeth I = 'Elizabeth the first'

Philip II = 'Philip the second'

Henry VIII = 'Henry the eighth'

47

3 Listen again. Use words from the first vocabulary box and the one below to complete the summary.

apartheid (a political system in which people of different races were separated)			
equal rights	**non-violent protest**	**courage**	**empire**
independence	**knowledge of the world**	**freedom**	**peace**

a Mahatma Gandhi was a ***civil rights activist*** who believed in ***non-violent protest*** and helped to bring about ***independence*** for India and .... from British rule.

b Nelson Mandela was a remarkable man and an excellent .... His leadership brought an end to .... in South Africa and gave .... to all South Africans.

c Ibn Battuta was an .... and a traveller who made a big contribution to ....

d Elizabeth I was a strong and popular ruler who brought 40 years of .... to England.

e Through her .... and determination, Rosa Parks helped to change the way black people were treated in the United States.

f Napoleon made himself .... of France in 1804 and by 1812, the Napoleonic .... included Spain, Italy and other countries in continental Europe.

Use of English
Past continuous

Remember that we use the past continuous and the past simple together to show that one action interrupted another.

*We **were doing** a project at school about great explorers when I **came across** a story about Ibn Battuta.*

We also use the past continuous for actions and situations that lasted for a short or limited time in the past.

*I learned a lot about people like Gandhi when I **was studying** history at university.*

Note the question forms:

*What **were** they **doing**? They were doing a project about great explorers.*

***Was** she **studying** English at university? No, she wasn't. She was studying history.*

4 Use the correct tense – past simple or past continuous – of the verbs in brackets to complete this text about Gandhi.

Mahatma Gandhi was born in India in 1869. His first job was as a lawyer in South Africa. While he .... (*live*) in South Africa, he .... (*have*) several bad experiences. For example, a police officer .... (*kick*) him when he .... (*walk*) on a footpath because only white people were allowed to walk there. On another occasion, when he .... (*travel*) on a train, he .... (*have*) to sit on the floor and he was beaten when he refused. When his job finished, he .... (*stay*) on in South Africa to help other Indians who .... (*protest*) about a law that would not allow them to vote in elections.

Speaking

5 Look at the people on the previous page. In your opinion, who is the most interesting and why?

7.2 The hidden pharaoh

In this lesson you will...

- read an account of a historical figure
- learn and use vocabulary to discuss a historical figure.

- **We can read about people who lived a long time ago. What other ways are there to find out about historical figures?**

Key words: History

c. (from Latin *circa* meaning 'about')
co-ruler
heir
expedition
obelisk
peace
pharaoh
prosperity
reign
throne
tomb
war

Reading

1 **Read the magazine article. The photos on these pages were used to illustrate the article. One shows Hatshepsut. What do the others show?**

2 **Answer the questions.**

a Of which country was Hatshepsut the ruler?
b Look at the sentence which begins 'In theory …' in paragraph 1. Who are 'he' and 'she' in this sentence?
c What sort of person do you think Hatshepsut was?
d How does the article show the importance of archaeology?

Speaking

3 **Work in pairs. Use the words in the history key words box to talk about Hatshepsut's life and what she did.**

4 **Work in groups. Discuss this question. Why do you think Hatshepsut wanted to be shown as a male pharaoh?**

Speaking tip

Notice the pronunciation of these words:

pharaoh: pronounced 'fair-oh'

reign: the same as 'rain'

heir: the same as 'air'

tomb: pronounced 'toom'

Notice how to say 'Thutmose I, II, III': 'Thutmose the first, second, third'.

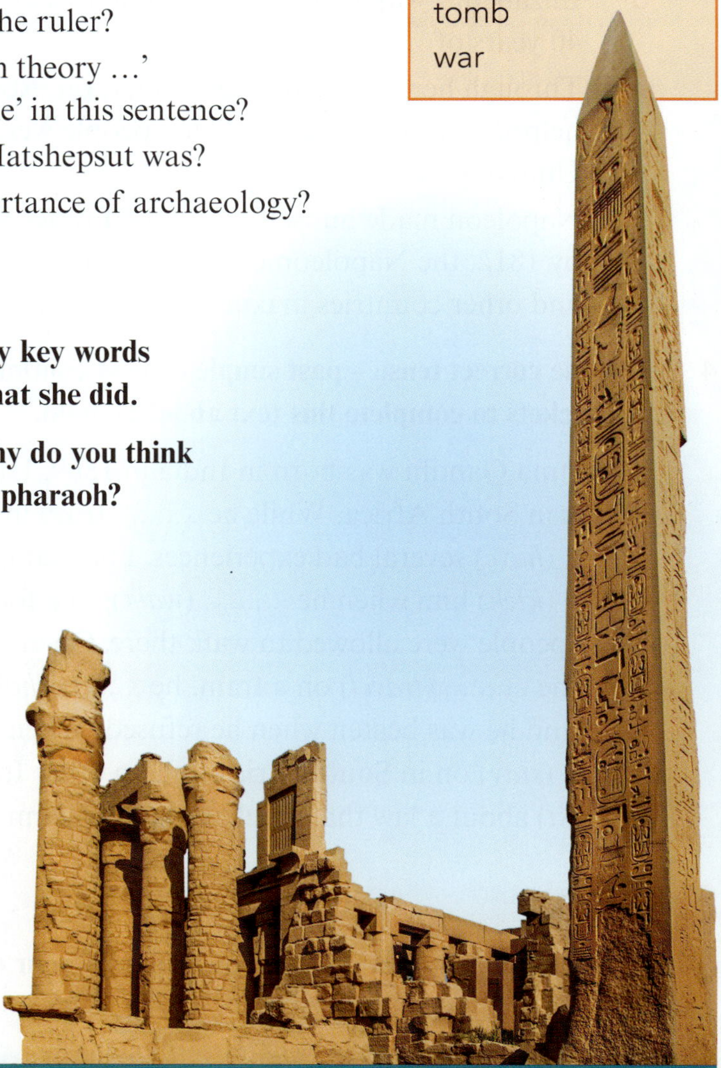

Hatshepsut, a pharaoh rediscovered

Hatshepsut (*c.* 1508–1458 BCE) was the daughter of a pharaoh, Thutmose I, and the wife of another pharaoh, Thutmose II. When Thutmose II died in 1479 BCE, Hapshepsut's young stepson, Thutmose III, was made his heir. However, just before Thutmose III was old enough to become the pharaoh, Hatshepsut declared herself pharaoh. In theory, he was her co-ruler, but in practice, she made the decisions. At her request, she was sometimes shown in statues and paintings as a male pharaoh.

Hatshepsut was more interested in trade than in war. She sent her soldiers on an expedition along the southern shore of the Red Sea to a land called Punt (possibly modern-day Eritrea). They returned with gold, ivory and unusual animals such as apes, panthers and giraffes. Hatshepsut was also responsible for several grand building projects, including two obelisks at Karnak and a temple in the hills behind Deir el-Bahri, in which she was buried. One of the obelisks still stands at Karnak, the tallest in Egypt at 30 metres high. It was carved from a single piece of stone. In the Temple of Hatshepsut, painted stone carvings show how the obelisk was carried on a barge down the River Nile. There are also scenes from the expedition to Punt, including men carrying trees in baskets to be replanted back in Egypt.

Her 21-year reign was a time of peace and prosperity for Egypt. When she died, Thutmose III at last had the throne to himself. Later in his reign, he began to erase Hatshepsut from the historical record, destroying the images of her as a male pharoah and removing her name from the list of kings. She disappeared from history for over 3000 years.

It was only when archaeologists began to work at Deir el-Bahri in 1822 and when they found her tomb in 1903 that a true picture of Egypt's female pharaoh began to be seen.

7.3 Who will be remembered?

In this lesson you will...

- listen to and role-play an interview about the achievements of a leader
- use verbs followed by prepositions.

- **Name a country. Ask other members of the class to say who the leader is.**

Jacinda Ardern became Prime Minister of New Zealand in 2017 at the age of 37. People have described her as the most powerful woman in the Southern Hemisphere and one of the most powerful women in the world.

Listening

48

1 **Listen to the podcast and write a caption for each of the photos.**

2 **Work in pairs. With a partner, say why the two girls in the interview think Jacinda Ardern will be remembered. Use the following notes to help you. Listen again and add detail to the notes.**

Prime Minister	Covid-19 pandemic
age 37	acted quickly (borders, strict rules)
re-elected	respect
ordinary people	climate change
children, schools, health service	people in Fiji, damage, rising sea levels

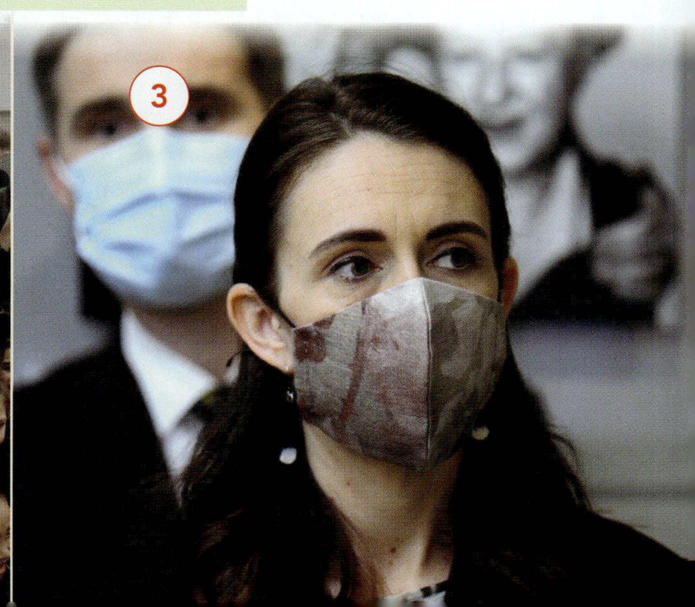

Use of English Verbs followed by prepositions

Some verbs are followed by prepositions. You know a lot of them already, like ***look at***, ***listen to***, ***think about***. Here is an example from the podcast you heard in Exercise 1.

Jacinda Ardern ***succeeded in*** *becoming Prime Minister at 37.*

You can succeed *in doing something* and you can succeed *in an exam*.

48

3 Complete these sentences with the correct prepositions. Then listen and check.

a People voted *for* her because she believed .... making things better for ordinary people.

b She said that there should be a health service you can rely ....

c She dealt .... the Covid-19 pandemic really well.

d Do you think people respected her .... that?

e She acted quickly to prevent the virus .... spreading.

f She insisted .... doing something about climate change.

g Her government has given money to help Fiji recover .... the damage caused by extreme weather conditions and rising sea levels, and to protect them .... these things in the future.

h Protecting the environment is important because New Zealand depends .... its agriculture.

Speaking

4 Work in small groups. Discuss this question.

One of the people in the podcast said that she thinks that Jacinda Ardern wants New Zealand 'to be on the right side of history'. What do you think this means?

Speaking tip

Here are some 'discourse markers'. (You heard them all in the interview in Exercise 1.) They will help your conversation sound natural. Use them in your interview in Exercise 5.

Well,	Oh yes,
Now,	Certainly.
Basically,	Right,
For example,	In fact,

5 Work in small groups. Choose a person who you think will be remembered in 50 years' time. Role-play a podcast interview about this person, like the interview in Exercise 1.

A: ***Who do you think will be remembered in 50 years' time?***

B: ***Well, if I had to choose one person, I would choose …***

A: ***Why?***

B: ***Basically, because …***

7.4 Creating and performing

In this lesson you will...

- learn about and discuss famous artists, musicians and writers
- use the past perfect simple.

- **Apart from political figures, which other historical figures do we remember, and why?**

Art
artist
painter
painting
sculptor
sculpture

Music
musician
composer
composition
performer
performance

Literature
author
poet
poetry, poem
novelist
novel
dramatist
drama, play

Listening

49

1 **Listen to the class discussing the question above. Use the words in the vocabulary box to say who each of the following people were.**

Frida Kahlo
Vincent Van Gogh
Claude Monet
Leonardo da Vinci
Michelangelo
Shen Zhou
Wolfgang Amadeus Mozart
Ludwig van Beethoven
William Shakespeare
Mary Shelley
Matsuo Bashō

2 **Listen again. What reasons do the students give for why the people mentioned are remembered?**

a Frida Kahlo and Van Gogh
b Monet
c Mozart and Beethoven
d Matsuo Bashō

Old pond
leap-splash –
a frog.
Matsuo Bashō

Reading

3 Read the extract about Mozart. What was special about him?

Wolfgang Amadeus Mozart was born in 1756 in Salzburg. At the age of four, he was already performing pieces on the harpsichord. He had watched his older sister Maria playing and soon started to play himself. At the age of five, he was composing his own music. By the age of seven, he had played at the court in Munich and at the imperial court in Vienna.

By the time Mozart was ten, he had already written works for piano, violin and orchestra. He had toured Europe and he had played in all the great concert halls in Paris, London, Brussels and Luxembourg. Everyone wanted to go to his performances because they had heard about the young genius.

When Mozart died in 1791, at the age of 35, he was composing his *Requiem*, a large work for voices and orchestra to remember the dead. Sadly, he hadn't finished it, so the *Requiem* was completed by his pupil, Süssmayr. It became one of Mozart's best-known compositions. Had he reached the height of his career? We shall never know.

4 Read the extract again and answer these questions.

a Which of the words in the vocabulary box in Exercise 1 apply to Mozart?

b Find two words in the text that mean the same as 'compositions'. One is used for short compositions; the other is used for longer compositions.

5 Complete the text by writing the verbs in the past perfect.

By the time Yuja Wang was 14, she .... (*already / study*) for seven years at Beijing's Central Conservatory of Music.

Her breakthrough came when she replaced the world-famous Argentinian pianist Martha Argerich, who .... (*cancel*) her appearances with the Boston Symphony Orchestra due to illness.

Yuja Wang played Tchaikovsky's *Piano Concerto No.1*. She .... (*not / play*) with the orchestra before, but her performance was so good that she received a standing ovation. By the end of the series, she .... (*make*) her name as a star of the classical music scene.

Speaking

6 Think of someone you know or have read about who achieved success at an early age. Write a sentence beginning:
By the time … was … , he / she had …* or *By the age of … , he / she had …

Tell the class about the person you have chosen.

Use of English
Past perfect simple

We use the past perfect when we are already talking about the past and we want to refer to an earlier past time.

had + past participle

*He **had watched** his older sister playing and soon started playing himself.*

(He watched his older sister playing. Then, later, he started playing himself.)

We often use the past perfect with expressions such as *by the time*.

*By the time Mozart was ten, he **had** already **written** works for piano, violin and orchestra.*

Negative

*He **hadn't finished** his* Requiem.

Questions

***Had** he **reached** the height of his career?*

7.5 The Islamic Golden Age

In this lesson you will...

- learn about the Islamic Golden Age
- find out about another important period of history.

Key words: History

BCE (before the Common Era)

(the 9th) century

c. (from Latin *circa* meaning 'about')

CE (the Common Era)

- **If you could go back in time, where and when would you go back to? Give your reasons.**

Reading

1 **Read the text. What do these people have in common?**

There are periods of history when civilisations make rapid progress in terms of knowledge and creativity. The **Islamic Golden Age** is one of them. Others include ancient Egypt, ancient Greece, the Roman empire, the Mayan civilisation, the Han dynasty, the European Renaissance, the Ottoman empire and the Mughal empire.

The Islamic Golden Age

The Islamic Golden Age began around 800 CE. Libraries and other centres of learning were established in many cities. The **House of Wisdom** (Bayt al-Hikma), for example, was founded in Baghdad at the beginning of the 9th century. It had 400,000 books.

The astrolabe

Mathematician **al-Khwarizmi** (*c.*780–850) was one of the most important scholars at the House of Wisdom and studied both Greek and Indian scientific texts. He is considered to be the inventor of algebra. He explained the process of balancing both sides of an equation. In about 820, he described the use of the astrolabe, which was an instrument for observing the position of the stars.

Ibn Sina

Ibn Sina (*c.*980–1037) was born in Uzbekistan. From an early age, he was interested in medicine. He said that by the age of 16, he had already successfully treated some patients. He wrote a medical handbook in five volumes, which was used as a textbook in European medical schools for almost 400 years.

Al-Razi

al-Razi (*c.*865–925) was from Persia. He went to Baghdad, where he worked as a doctor and was the director of two hospitals. He kept notes about his patients and their symptoms, and developed the idea of doing experiments to discover new treatments.

Omar Khayyam

Omar Khayyam (1048–1131) was a Persian mathematician and astronomer. He was the first to describe how to use geometry to solve cubic equations. He also calculated the length of the year as 365.24219858156 days, more precisely than anyone had calculated it before. By the time he was 25, he had written many treatises on astronomy and mathematics. He was also a poet.

2 Find the words for the following in the text:

- **a** someone who is good at maths
- **b** someone who studies a subject and knows a lot about it (*Clue: it's similar to the word 'school'*)
- **c** a type of maths that uses numbers, letters and symbols. For example: $\sqrt{2x + 3y}$
- **d** $x^3 - 9x = 0$
- **e** where you study if you want to be a doctor
- **f** a type of maths to do with shape and size. For example:

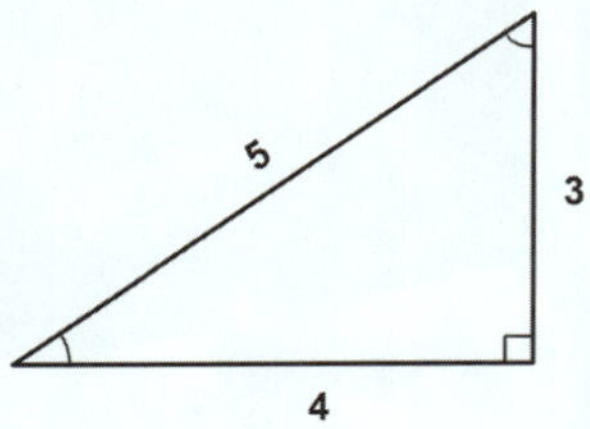

- **g** to find the answer to a problem, especially a maths problem
- **h** someone who studies the stars
- **i** the study of the stars

3 Work in pairs. Read the text again. Then take turns to ask each other five questions.

Student A: Look at the text and choose five questions to ask, like this:

Where was the House of Wisdom?

Student B: Answer student A's questions without looking at the text.
Then ask student A a question:

How many books were there in the House of Wisdom?

Speaking

4 Discuss these questions.

- **a** How are the historical figures described in the text different from the people you read about in Lessons 7.1–7.3?
- **b** Why do you think there was an Islamic Golden Age from 800 CE?
- **c** If someone asked you, 'What did you learn in your English lesson today?', what would you say?

5 Find out more. Find out about one of the other periods of history mentioned in the introduction to the text. Who were the important historical figures in that period? Write a paragraph about them, like the ones about people in the Islamic Golden Age.

Bin Biao (3–54 CE) was a historian in the Han Dynasty. He wrote …

7.6 Leonardo in 3D

In this lesson you will...

- listen to and report a conversation about an unusual exhibition
- talk about and report what you've seen, read and done recently.

- **What kinds of art do you like best, and why?**

The European Renaissance was a golden age for Italy. It produced artists such as Leonardo da Vinci and Michelangelo, whose paintings became known throughout the world. Leonardo was not only a painter but also a sculptor and an inventor. His work was shown in an unusual exhibition in Milan, Italy, to mark the 500th anniversary of his death.

Listening

50

1 **Listen to Claudia and her friend Lauren talking about the Leonardo da Vinci 3D exhibition. What did Claudia think of it?**

50

2 Listen again. True or false?

- **a** Both girls have been to the exhibition.
- **b** There were sculptures in the exhibition.
- **c** At the exhibition there was a hologram of the artist.
  (A hologram is an image that appears to be solid and have depth when light shines on it in a particular way.)
- **d** Leonardo da Vinci was an inventor as well as an artist.
- **e** You could see holograms of some of the things da Vinci designed.
- **f** You were allowed to take photos at the exhibition.

Use of English Past perfect in reported speech

When you are reporting what someone said, you often have to change the tense. If someone uses the present perfect, you change it to the past perfect when you report what they said:

Claudia: 'I've been busy.'

Claudia said she'd been busy. (she'd = she had)

'I haven't seen the real things.'

She said she hadn't seen the real things. (she hadn't = she had not)

Complete this sentence:

In reported speech, we change *have / has* to …

Questions

Lauren: 'Where have you been?'

Lauren asked Claudia where she'd been.

Remember to use *if* when you report *yes / no* questions.

Claudia: 'Have you seen any of his inventions?'

Claudia asked Lauren if she had seen any of his inventions.

We also change the past simple to the past perfect in reported speech:

Lauren: 'Did you take any pictures?'

Lauren asked Claudia if she had taken any pictures.

3 Report these statements from the conversation.

- **a** Lauren (to Claudia): I haven't seen you for ages.
  Lauren said she hadn't seen her for ages.
- **b** Claudia: I've just been to the most fantastic exhibition.
- **c** Lauren: I've read about him.
- **d** Lauren: Has the exhibition finished?
- **e** Lauren: I haven't heard much about it.

Speaking

4 Work in pairs. Ask and answer. Make notes of your partner's answers.

- **a** What have you seen at the cinema or on TV recently?
- **b** What have you read recently? Tell me about it.
- **c** Have you been anywhere interesting recently? Where have you been?
- **d** Have you ever been to an exhibition?
- **e** Have you seen any famous paintings, sculptures or other works of art in real life?

5 Change partners. Tell your new partner what your first partner said.

7.7 Improve your writing

In this lesson you will...

- write a short biography of a historical figure.

1 Look at the photo. Answer the questions.

a What is happening in this photo?

b What do you think had happened just before it was taken?

c What do you think is going to happen?

2 Read the biography of Rosa Parks. What can you say about the photograph now?

3 Read about Rosa Parks. Work in pairs. Answer these questions.

a Which paragraph gives you biographical details about Rosa Parks' early life?

b Which paragraph tells you about what life was like at the time – the historical background to the story?

c Which paragraph describes a key event in her life?

d Which sentences tell you about Rosa Parks' achievements?

e Why do you think the writer quotes Rosa Parks?

f Why is it important, in this kind of writing, to give historical background as well as facts about someone's life and achievements?

4 Work individually or in groups. Choose a historical figure to write about.

- Include biographical details, historical background and achievements.
- The easiest way to organise your material is chronologically, that is, in the order in which things happen.

5 Write a short biography.

- Plan your work in paragraphs.
- Write a draft. Include some time phrases.
- Check each other's work for mistakes before writing a final version.

6 Check your writing.

- Which time phrases did you include?
- Compare your draft with your final version. What did you change, and why?

10 **segregation:** separating people into groups, such as by race.

22 **campaign:** to take part in organised activities with the aim of changing something in society

39 **arrest:** to take someone prisoner because they are suspected of having done something wrong

41 **boycott:** to refuse to do something as a way of showing you think it is wrong

53 **racial injustice:** unfair treatment because of a person's race

Writing tip

Use time phrases to give a clear sense of the sequence of events in your text. Find these time phrases in the text:

In 1913

At the age of

In those days

In the 1940s

At that time

On 1 December 1955

Eventually

for the rest of her life

Rosa Parks was born in Tuskegee, Alabama in the USA in 1913. At the age of 11, she moved with her mother to live near the state capital, Montgomery, where she attended high school. She had to leave early, at 16, to look after her grandmother and then also her mother.

When Rosa was growing up, the southern states, including Alabama, had passed laws that reduced the rights of black people. There was racial segregation, which meant that black people could not use the same public places (such as schools, churches, libraries, restaurants and toilets), as white people. Public transport had separate sections for black passengers. In those days, there were no school buses for black children. They had to walk to school. In her autobiography, Rosa remembers that she was frequently bullied by white children in her neighbourhood and had to learn to stand up for herself from an early age.

In the 1940s, Rosa Parks became an activist in the civil rights movement and started to campaign for black people to have the same rights as white people. At that time, she worked in a variety of jobs, as a housekeeper, in a hospital, and as a shop assistant. On 1 December 1955, after a hard day's work in a department store in Montgomery, she got on a bus to go home, paid her fare and sat in the section for black passengers. As the bus travelled along its regular route, all of the seats for white people filled up. The bus driver noticed that some white passengers were standing, because all the seats at the front (the seats for white people) were taken. He stopped the bus and asked four black passengers, including Rosa Parks, to give up their seats so that the white people could sit down. Rosa Parks refused to give up her seat. The bus driver called the police and she was arrested.

Following Rosa Park's arrest, plans were made for black people to boycott Montgomery's bus service. Some people shared cars to get to work; others walked. The boycott lasted 381 days. It was a problem for the bus companies because there were around 40,000 commuters not using the buses, so the companies lost a lot of money. Eventually, the US Supreme Court ruled that segregation on the city's buses was wrong, and Montgomery changed its law.

Rosa Parks became known as 'the mother of the civil rights movement' for refusing to obey a law that was unjust. She continued to campaign against racial injustice for the rest of her life.

'I would like to be remembered as a person who wanted to be free ... so that other people would also be free.' *Rosa Parks*

Rosa Parks (in the centre) riding on a bus after the US Supreme Court ruled that segregation on the buses was wrong

7.8 Project challenge

Project 1: People who made a difference

You're going to give a presentation about a historical figure.

1 Work in groups. Who will you choose to be your historical figure?

2 Find out about the person you've chosen. Each person in the group takes a different aspect to research, for example:

Biographical details

Historical background

Achievements

3 Prepare your presentation slides. Give each one a heading.

Marie Curie – early years

Life in Paris

Research – scientific work

Nobel prizes

4 Decide who is going to present each slide. Then give your presentation.

- Remember that you can use time phrases, like the ones in the Writing tip box in Lesson 7.7, to make the sequence of events clear.
- You can summarise what someone has just said before going on to talk about your own slide.
  As Alisha has just said, …
- Make links to what others have said:
  You remember that Idris told us that …

- What did you learn from doing this project?
- When you gave your presentation, what was the value of making links to what someone else had said?

Project 2: An interview with a historical figure

You're going to write an interview with a historical figure.

1 Work in groups. Each group imagines they are going to meet a famous person from history. Decide on the person.

2 Write the questions you would ask in the interview.

3 How would he/she reply to your questions? Look up some information about the person's life.

4 Use your questions and the information you have found to write a short dialogue, lasting no more than a minute. It can be serious or comic, like this one:

An interview with Elizabeth I

Q: Good afternoon, Your Majesty.

A: Good afternoon. Now, you have some questions for me.

Q: Yes, umm, have you been to the theatre recently?

A: Yes, I have. I've seen two plays by a young writer. I think his name is William Shakespeare.

Q: Did you enjoy them?

A: Yes, they were very good. There was one called *The Comedy of Errors*. It was very amusing.

Q: And have you had any interesting visitors lately?

A: Yes, I have, actually. I've had a visit from Sir Francis Drake. He's a sailor, you know. He's been all over the world. He gave me a beautiful piece of jewellery. It's made of gold with a diamond in the middle of it.

Q: Which is your favourite palace, Your Majesty?

A: Well, I was born in Greenwich Palace, but I didn't like it much. I spent my childhood at Hatfield Palace. But the one I like best is Whitehall Palace. It's very convenient because it's in the centre of London.

5 Role-play your conversation in front of the other groups. They must listen very carefully!

6 Ask the class questions to see what they remember about your conversation.

What did we ask the queen first?

You asked her if she had been to the theatre recently. She said she had seen two plays …

- What did you learn about the person you chose?
- How did you choose whether to write a serious dialogue or a comic one? Which is more difficult to do?

7.9 Fiction

War Horse, by Michael Morpurgo, is the story of a horse. He becomes separated from the boy who owns him when he is sold to the cavalry (the group of soldiers who ride horses) in the First World War (1914–1918). The boy's and the horse's experience of war are at the heart of the book, which has been made into a play and a film.

51

1 First, listen to the extract from *War Horse*. Answer these questions.

- **a** Who is the narrator (the 'I')?
- **b** Who is Albert?
- **c** Who is Joey?
- **d** Who is Zoey?

2 Now read and listen to the extract again. Answer these questions.

- **a** How does Joey's attitude to Albert change?
- **b** How are Albert and his father different?
- **c** How does Albert create 'a bond of trust and affection' (*lines 29–30*) with Joey?
- **d** In the first three paragraphs, which words and phrases create a positive, calm and quiet atmosphere?
- **e** How many verbs to do with the sense of touch can you find?

3 Work in groups. Discuss these questions.

- **a** In Unit 7, which historical figures have been seen on horseback? (Try to answer without looking back!)
- **b** Do you think there is a special bond between people and horses? Why / Why not?
- **c** Why did people value horses in the past? Why do they value them now?

Albert was about the same height as me and talked so gently as he approached that I was immediately calmed and not a little intrigued, and so stood where I was against the wall. I jumped at first when he touched me, but could see at once that he meant me no harm. He smoothed my back first and then my neck, talking all the while about what a fine time we would have together, how I would grow up to be the smartest horse in the whole wide world, and how we would go out hunting together.

After a bit he began to rub me gently with his coat. He rubbed me until I was dry and then dabbed salted water onto my face where the skin had been rubbed raw. He brought in some sweet hay and a bucket of cool, deep water. I do not believe he stopped talking all the time. As he turned to go out of the stable I called out to him to thank him and he seemed to understand for he smiled broadly and stroked my nose.

"We'll get along, you and I," he said kindly. "I shall call you Joey, only because it rhymes with Zoey, and then maybe, yes maybe because it suits you. I'll be out again in the morning – and don't worry, I'll look after you. I promise you that. Sweet dreams, Joey."

"You should never talk to horses, Albert," said his mother from outside. "They never understand you. They're stupid creatures. Obstinate and stupid, that's what your father says, and he's known horses all his life."

"Father just doesn't understand them," said Albert. "I think he's frightened of them."

I went over to the door and watched Albert and his mother walking away and up into the darkness. I knew then that I had found a friend for life, that there was an instinctive and immediate bond of trust and affection between us. Next to me old Zoey leant over her door to try to touch me, but our noses would not quite meet.

[3] **intrigued:** very interested

[5] **he meant me no harm:** he wasn't going to hurt me

[5] **smooth:** to move your hand across something to make it flat

[9] **rub:** to press and move your hand, a cloth or an object over a surface

[10] **dab:** to touch something gently several times with a cloth

[11] **raw:** skin that is red and painful because it has been rubbed too much

[11] **hay:** dry grass

[12] **bucket:** a large container for carrying water

[13] **stable:** a place to keep horses

[14] **smile broadly:** to give a big smile

[15] **stroke:** to gently move your hand over something

[16] **get along:** to get on well

[18] **it suits you:** it's right for you

[22] **obstinate:** not willing to change your ideas

[28] **instinctive:** natural

[28] **bond of trust:** an understanding that each will always be true to the other

Joey goes to war. During the first autumn of the war, in 1914, he is given to Trooper Warren to ride. (A 'trooper' is an ordinary soldier.) On the next page, the second extract from *War Horse* tells us about Trooper Warren.

4 Read and listen to the second extract. Has Trooper Warren already ridden into battle? How do you know?

… he had been an apprentice blacksmith with his father. Then the war had broken out. He did not want to join up, he said; but the squire of the village had spoken to his father and his father, who rented his house and his smithy from the squire, had no option but to send him off to war, and since he had grown up around horses he volunteered to join the cavalry.

"I tell you, Joey," he said one evening as he was picking out my hooves, "I'll tell you I never thought I would get on a horse again after that first battle … it was just the idea of riding a horse again that terrified the life out of me. Wouldn't think that possible, would you? Not with me being a smithy and all. Still, I'm over it now and you've done that for me Joey. Given me back my confidence. Feel I can do anything now. Feel like one of those knights in armour when I'm up on you."

[1] apprentice: someone who is learning to do a particular job

[1] blacksmith: someone who makes and repairs things made of iron, especially horseshoes

[2] join up: to go into the army

[3] squire: in the past, a man who owned most of the land around a village

[4] smithy: the place where a blacksmith works (or an abbreviation of 'blacksmith')

[4] had no option but to: had no choice apart from

[7] picking out my hooves: getting the stones and dirt from a horse's feet (hooves)

[10] terrify: to make someone feel very frightened

[13] knights: in the past, men of high social position trained to fight as soldiers on horses

[13] armour: metal clothes that soldiers wore in the past

5 Work in pairs. Answer these questions.

a Trooper Warren's father, after the squire had spoken to him, felt that he had to send his son to fight in the war. Why? What do you think the squire said to him?

b Why do you think Trooper Warren talks to Joey?

Writing

6 The author, Michael Morpurgo, chose not to write what the squire said to Trooper Warren's father, or what his father said to Trooper Warren. Imagine he had decided to write the conversations. What would he have written?

Conversation 1

'Good morning, Mr Warren.'

'Good morning, squire.'

'Now, Mr Warren, … '

Conversation 2

'Son, I need to talk to you.'

'Yes, father.'

'Right, well, …'

Check your progress

General knowledge quiz

How much do you remember about what you've learned?

1 Why is Mahatma Gandhi considered to be the 'father of the Indian nation'?

2 Who was queen of England from 1558 to 1603?

3 He became emperor of France in 1804. His empire included Italy and Spain, as well as France. What was his name?

4 Who was Hatshepsut?

5 It's 30 metres high, it's made of a single piece of stone, it has a point at the top, it's at Karnak, in Egypt, and it's called Hatshepsut's … .
(Here are the letters, mixed up: B E L S O K I)

6 Who is Jacinda Ardern?

7 What do Frida Kahlo, Claude Monet and Vincent Van Gogh have in common?

8 The House of Wisdom had 400,000 books. Where was it?

9 This is an astrolabe. What was it used for?

10 Why is Rosa Parks remembered today?

Vocabulary

1 **Put the words under the correct headings in the table.**

artist	composer	musician
poet	painting	sculpture
novel	dramatist	performer
piano	poetry	painter
play	harpsichord	novelist
violin	sculptor	writer

Art	Music	Literature
People ***artist***	*People*	*People*
What they create ***painting***	*What they play*	*What they write*

2 **Complete the sentences with the correct words from Exercise 1.**

a *Mona Lisa* is a .... by the artist, Leonardo da Vinci.

b At primary school, we learned a few poems by heart, but I don't read much .... now.

c *The Comedy of Errors* is a .... by William Shakespeare, the most famous Elizabethan dramatist.

d Pinar Toprak writes music for films. She's the .... of music for the film *Captain Marvel.*

e I like works in 3D, so I prefer .... to painting.

Use of English

1 Put the verbs into the correct tense, past simple or past continuous.

a We .... (*need*) to look at several websites because we .... (*plan*) a trip around New Zealand.
We needed to look at several websites because we were planning a trip around New Zealand.

b I .... (*just / fall*) asleep when I .... (*hear*) the doorbell ring.

c .... (*you / go*) to the sports centre when I .... (*see*) you?

d Sorry. I .... (*not / know*) you .... (*wait*) for me.

e What .... (*you / watch*) on TV when I .... (*call*)?

2 Choose the correct preposition.

a You can't always rely ***with / on*** the information on a website.

b Who are you going to vote ***for / on*** in the school council election?

c Don't come to school until you've recovered ***from / of*** the virus.

d I don't know what time we'll arrive. It depends ***on / of*** the traffic.

e Sorry, I'm really busy. I can't deal ***about / with*** that at the moment.

3 Put the verbs into the correct tense, past simple or past perfect.

a I (*not / play*) for a long time, so I (*not / win*) the tennis match.
I hadn't played for a long time, so I didn't win the tennis match.

b We .... (*arrive*) late, but luckily the concert .... (*not / start*) on time.

c .... (*you / see*) the play before or .... (*be*) this the first time?

d He .... (*miss*) the flight because he .... (*leave*) his passport at home.

4 Report these statements using the past perfect. Remember to make other changes where necessary.

a "I've bought a flute with my pocket money."
She said she had bought a flute with her pocket money.

b "I've found some family photos at the bottom of a drawer."
He said ....

c "Have you seen the new James Bond film?"
She asked me ....

d "I haven't had time to practise the guitar."
He said ....

Summary checklist

I can

- ☐ talk about interesting people in history.
- ☐ understand conversations about major figures in art and music.
- ☐ talk about someone who achieved success at an early age.
- ☐ ask and answer questions about important figures from the Islamic Golden Age.
- ☐ report a conversation about an art exhibition.
- ☐ write a short biography of a historical figure.

8 Storytelling

In this unit you will...

- **listen** to and **give** opinions about books and stories
- **read** about traditional stories and **discuss** them
- **talk** about your favourite stories from childhood
- **listen** to and **understand** the details of a story
- **reconstruct** a story from notes
- **read** and then **write** a summary of the first part of a traditional story
- **listen** to and **write** a summary of the second part of a traditional story
- **write** a short essay giving your opinions about what makes a good story
- **write** and **perform** a scene for a play
- **read** an Australian Aboriginal story
- **narrate** a story to an audience.

Getting started

“Storytelling has a long history. Why do you think people have always enjoyed telling and listening to stories?”

Watch this!

8.1 A good story

In this lesson you will...

- listen to and give opinions about books and stories
- use the present perfect with *ever, never, already, just, still* and *yet*.

science fiction ('sci-fi')
spy stories
historical fiction
real-life stories
thrillers
crime fiction
horror stories

- **When you're choosing a book to read, or a film to watch, what do you look for?**

Vocabulary

1 **Look at the books and read the captions. What kind of stories are they?**

a *a horror story*

a

In *The Monster in the Deep*, Laurie and his friend Josh investigate strange events in his village. Be prepared to be scared!

b

Secret Identity is one of a series of novels featuring 14-year-old spy Alice Steele.

c

Where Eagles Fly is set in 13th-century China.

d

The Amazing Trip to Planet Orb is about two boys and a homemade spaceship.

Listening

53

2 **You will hear some of these adjectives in Exercise 3. First, listen and repeat them. Why are they divided into the three columns? (Clue: think of where the stress falls on each of the words.)**

brilliant	amusing	realistic
complicated	descriptive	disappointing
interesting	enjoyable	
scary	exciting	
serious	imaginative	
	mysterious	
	surprising	

54

3 **Listen to four students talking about books they've enjoyed. What kind of stories does each person like?**

4 **Listen again. Why do the students like the books they mention?**

1 The first speaker says she likes … stories because they're …

55

5 **Listen to a conversation at a school book club and answer the questions.**

a Why had one of the students already started reading the book again?

b What did she mean when she said 'I couldn't put it down'?

c What do you know about the characters and main character in the story?

d Why was reading the story 'like going back in time'?

e Why did one of the students say 'Don't tell me what happens at the end'?

f What do you know about the way the story ends?

Use of English Present perfect with indefinite time adverbs

We use the present perfect with expressions that mean 'time up to now', like *ever*, *never*, and *still*.

*I've **never** read a book so quickly.*

*Have you **ever** done that?*

*She **still** hasn't finished the book.*

We also use the present perfect with words that mean 'close to now' like *already*, *just* and *yet*.

*I enjoyed the book so much that I've **already** started reading it again from the beginning!*

*The book we've **just** talked about is set in the 16th century.*

*I haven't finished reading it **yet**.*

What do you notice about the position of the adverbs in these sentences? Choose the correct options:

Put *yet* at the **beginning / end** of a sentence.

Put *never*, *already* and *just* **before / after** *have / has*.

Put *still* **before / after** *have / has*.

In questions, put *ever* **before / after** the past participle.

Speaking

6 **Work in pairs or small groups. Answer these questions. Make sure you use adverbs such as *already*, *yet* and *ever* in the correct position.**

a What was the last book you read?

b Which three adjectives from Exercise 2 would you use to describe a story you've just read or a film you've just seen?

c Have you ever read a whole book from start to finish in two days?

d I've never enjoyed a book so much! Which book would you say this about?

e Have you ever stopped reading a book or watching a film before the end? Why?

f Are there any books by your favourite author that you haven't read yet? What are they called?

8.2 Tales from around the world

In this lesson you will...

- read about traditional stories and discuss their appeal
- use a list of key words to summarise a text.

Key words: Literature

fable: a short story, often with animals as characters. It gives a moral message – a lesson about how people should or shouldn't behave

fairy tale: similar to a folk tale, but with magic and imaginary creatures such as fairies

folk tale: an old story that has been told many times, from generation to generation

legend: a story about people and events that is believed to be true

myth: a story about people or events, often including imaginary creatures and experiences

- **When do you enjoy listening to a story? When do you prefer reading one?**

Reading

1 **Choose a key word to describe each of the stories below.**

a

Slow and steady wins the race. The hare is sure he will win, but does he?

b

The soldier Bellerophon and his winged horse Pegasus meet the Chimera, a terrifying fire-breathing monster, with a snake's tail, a goat's body and a lion's head …

c

For 400 years, the Turkish people were trapped in the Ergenekon valley, until a wolf called Asena led them to freedom …

d

Cinderella goes to the ball in a beautiful dress provided by her fairy godmother, but she loses one of her shoes as she leaves.

2 **Read the text. What is used in storytelling traditions in addition to the spoken word?**

Every culture has its own stories – poems and rhymes, legends, myths, fables and folk tales. Before languages were written down, stories were told within families and communities, to entertain, inform and educate.

Storytelling, as a spoken tradition, is still popular. In West Africa, storytellers are called *griots*. They are the keepers of local history and tell stories about the ancestors of their people. They often play a stringed instrument called a *kora* to accompany their stories. The role of the *griot*, or *griotte* if the storyteller is a woman, is usually passed down in a family, from an older member to a younger one.

Shadow puppets, which are silhouettes made from leather or paper, tell folk stories and give moral messages. The people who make the shadow puppets move are called puppeteers. They sometimes sing the story or are accompanied by singers and musicians.

Shadow puppetry is an ancient art that is still popular in China, India, Indonesia, Malaysia and Thailand.

Shadow puppets

Zajal is a poetic battle between two speakers who recite verses in classical Arabic. The first speaker has to recite some lines of poetry, and then the opponent has to respond. It's like a modern-day rap battle, but it dates from the 12th century.

In Japan, a traditional storyteller called a *hanashika* sits alone on a stage and performs a monologue. The *hanashika* is a comedian who entertains listeners with amusing tales of everyday life while also giving moral messages and lessons to be learned from history.

Vocabulary

3 **Work in pairs. Find the following words in the text and explain them in your own words. Then use them to summarise the text.**

ancestors	to recite
stringed instrument	to respond
to accompany	monologue
silhouette	comedian
battle	

In West Africa, storytellers …

In China, India, Indonesia, Malaysia and Thailand, …

Zajal …

In Japan, …

Speaking

4 **Work in pairs or small groups. Discuss these questions.**

a Why do you think storytelling was popular in the past? Why do you think it's still popular today?

b Look back at the types of stories in Exercise 1. How many examples of each kind of story can you think of?

c Which kind of storytelling did you find most interesting? Why?

8.3 Stories we remember

In this lesson you will...

- talk about your favourite stories from childhood
- learn and use the present perfect continuous.

- **What kind of stories did you like listening to when you were younger?**

Listening

56

1 Listen to Nadya, Yousef and Amira talking about their favourite childhood stories. Match them to the book illustrations.

Nadya

Yousef

Amira

a

b

c

2 Listen again. Then answer the questions.

a What kind of stories did Yousef like when he was younger?

b What did he mean when he said that he got to know the story 'by heart'? Why had this happened?

c What kind of stories did Amira say she liked as a child?
d Why did she like the story she chose as her favourite?
e How did Nadya describe her favourite story?
f What is the story about?
g Why can she still remember the lines, 'Who's been eating my porridge?' and 'Who's been sleeping in my bed?'

Speaking

3 Work in pairs or small groups. Now it's your turn to talk about your favourite story. The rest of the group has to guess the title.

a What was your favourite story when you were younger?
b Why did you like it?
c What was it about?
d Who were the main characters? What were they like?
e Can you remember any of the words from the story?

Speaking tip

Make your speaking more expressive by adding words to qualify adjectives:

a little bit scary

not too predictable

absolutely fascinating

quite a simple story

Use of English Present perfect continuous

We use the present perfect continuous to talk about events or situations that started in the past and are continuing up to now.

have / has + been + -ing

*I**'ve** **been** **reading** the story to my younger brother recently.*

We use it to talk about past actions with results in the present.

*Who**'s** (Who **has**) **been** **sleeping** in my bed?*

(The speaker asks this question because he / she can see that the bed is untidy.)

4 Work in pairs. What have you been doing in this lesson? Use the prompts in the table to make answers that are true for you.

In this lesson, we've been talking about our favourite stories.

I We My partner	have / 've has / 's haven't hasn't	been	talking about discussing exchanging finding helping (me) looking out of thinking about working	stories a favourite story in pairs or groups ideas about children's books information on the internet the window to do this exercise football / friends / TV

8.4 A walk in the park

In this lesson you will...

- listen to and understand the details of a story
- reconstruct the story from your notes.

- **What makes a story exciting?**

Listening

57 **1 Listen to the story. Write down three adjectives to describe it.**

Vocabulary

2 Work in pairs. Match these words from the story with their definitions.

1	deserted	a	come nearer
2	(to) head for	b	empty
3	massive	c	go in the direction of
4	swiftly	d	large wild black cat
5	(to) approach	e	nervously
6	anxiously	f	quickly
7	panther	g	very big

3 Work in pairs or small groups. Read the questions. Then listen again and write notes for your answers.

a When does the story take place?
In January

b What was the weather like?

c Where were Adi and Taslin at the start of the story and what were they doing?

d When did they decide to go out and where to?

e What did they do before they left home?

f What was it like in the street outside their house?

g What did they see and what did they hear?

h What did they do when they reached the park?

i Why did they decide to start walking home?

j What did they see when they were walking along a path between some trees? What happened next?

k Why were the two people running, and what did they ask?

l How did Taslin and Adi feel when they got home?

m Why did their parents say, 'You've been reading too many horror stories'?

n What did they find out the following day?

Use of English Preposition + noun

Prepositions show how things are connected to each other:

time	***in*** January	purpose	(go) ***for*** a walk
	at 4 o'clock	direction	***along*** the path
	during the holidays		***towards*** the play area
place	***in*** the park	possession	***with*** a basketball hoop
	on a wall		***with*** bright yellow eyes

4 **Put the preposition in the correct place in each sentence.**

a It was a warm, sunny afternoon ***in*** July. (*in*)

b My friend, Jani, messaged me, asking if I wanted to go a swim. (*for*)

c We decided to go to the beach a lifeguard's station in the middle. (*with*)

d We agreed to meet 4 o'clock. (*at*)

e When I arrived, Jani was sitting a rock looking at the sea. (*on*)

f We swam the warm sea for half an hour. (*in*)

g Afterwards, as we walked the beach, the sun was beginning to go down over the sea. (*along*)

5 **Using your notes from Exercise 3, write sentences to reconstruct the story. Include words from Exercise 2. Then read your story to the class. Listen to the other groups' versions of the story. Add any missing details to your version.**

Speaking and writing

6 **Work in pairs or small groups. Write your own story by adapting the story in Exercise 1.**

First plan your story using the questions in Exercise 3. Start like this:

When did the story take place? In June.

What was the weather like? It was warm and sunny.

Writing tip

Add detail and variety to your writing.

- Use adjectives to set the scene.
  *It was a **cold, grey** day in January. The street was **deserted**.*
- Give detail to create a picture and sound.
  The wind blew a few dry leaves and an empty can down the middle of the road.
- Use time expressions to show the order of events.
  At about 4 o'clock
  After a while
- Use a variety of words to avoid repeating verbs like *said*:
  *she **asked**, he **called out**, they **replied**, he **shouted**, she **whispered**, I **cried**.*
- Use a variety of words to describe coming and going.
  *We **followed** the path*
  *We **reached** the play area*
  *We decided to **head for** home*
  *It was **moving** swiftly*
  *It was **approaching** very fast*

8.5 Aladdin: a traditional story

In this lesson you will...

- read and then write a summary of the first part of a traditional story.

- **Why do you think some stories from a long time ago are still popular today?**

The One Thousand and One Nights is a collection of folk stories written in Arabic, dating as far back as the 10th century. *Aladdin* was not in the original manuscript. It was added later, in the 18th century, by Antoine Galland, who translated all the stories from Arabic into French. Since then, it has appeared in many books, on stage and in films.

Reading

1 Read the first part of the story of Aladdin. Who are the main characters?

Once upon a time, there lived in a city in China a poor tailor who had a son called Aladdin. When Aladdin was ten, his father wanted to teach him to be a tailor, but he didn't like sewing and making clothes. He was a lazy boy, and he preferred playing with his friends.

Aladdin's father died, and his mother began spinning cotton to earn money. One day, while Aladdin was playing in the street, a man approached Aladdin and said 'At last I have found you!'

'Who are you?' asked Aladdin.

'I am your father's brother. I knew you were his son the moment I saw you. You're just like him.'

'But my father is dead, sir,' said Aladdin.

'Oh no!' said the man. 'Then I am too late.' And he began to cry. 'Here, take these, my boy,' he said, and gave Aladdin ten gold coins. 'Give these to your mother and tell her that I should like to visit her tomorrow. Go now.'

Aladdin ran like the wind and told his mother about the man. 'He'd like to visit us tomorrow,' he said.

'What are you talking about, Aladdin? Your father has no brothers living.'

'But, mother, he said that he wanted to come to see us tomorrow.'

The man came to the house and told the story of how he had been away for many years, and that he was heartbroken to hear that his brother was dead. Aladdin's mother was so moved by the man's tears that she believed his story. Neither she nor Aladdin realised that the man was in fact a sorcerer from Morocco.

The sorcerer offered to help Aladdin to become a silk merchant and have a shop of his own. Aladdin and his mother were delighted. He took Aladdin to the market and bought him a fine suit of clothes.

The following day, the sorcerer took Aladdin to a beautiful garden. In the garden, he showed him a big marble stone.

'Under that stone there is treasure that belongs to you, Aladdin. Come, lift the stone.'

'But uncle,' Aladdin replied, 'I am not strong enough.'

'Do as I say,' said the sorcerer.

Aladdin used all his strength. The stone moved easily and Aladdin saw some steps down into a cave.

'Go down into the cave,' said the sorcerer. 'You will see all sorts of treasures. Keep going until you see a lamp. Bring back this lamp and you will be the richest man on earth. Here, this ring will help you if you are in danger. It will protect you. Don't lose it.' He took a ring from his finger and gave it to Aladdin.

Aladdin went down into the cave, past the treasures and found the lamp. He took the lamp, and on the way back to the opening of the cave he helped himself to some of the treasure. But the entrance of the cave was so high that Aladdin could not climb out. 'Help me, uncle!' he shouted.

'Give me the lamp first,' the sorcerer replied.

'I cannot,' said Aladdin. 'Just give me your hand to help me up, and then you can have the lamp.'

The sorcerer became impatient and, thinking that Aladdin wanted to keep the lamp for himself, he made the marble stone move back into place by using a magic charm. Aladdin was imprisoned in the cave.

The sorcerer knew that the lamp would make the person who owned it a very rich man, but he was afraid that Aladdin would cheat him, so he made sure that he could not escape.

Aladdin shouted and shouted, but no help came. At the end of three days without food or drink, he had given up hope when he happened to rub the ring that the sorcerer had given him. At once a genie appeared.

'I am here, master!' the genie said. 'Your wish is my command.'

Aladdin was terrified, but he remembered what the sorcerer had said about the ring.

'Take me back home,' said Aladdin, and the next thing he knew he was back at his mother's house.

His mother cried with joy when she saw him. Aladdin now realised that the man who had given him the ring was not his uncle, but an evil sorcerer.

2 Answer these questions.

a In which country is the story set? A second country is mentioned. Why?
b What does this extract tell you about Aladdin's parents?
c Aladdin met a man in the street.
Who did the man pretend to be?
d Why did the man take Aladdin to the cave and what did he tell him to do?
e Why couldn't Aladdin get out of the cave?
f The man gave Aladdin a ring. How was it useful?
g The genie says, 'Your wish is my command.'
What does this mean?
h What did Aladdin tell the genie to do?
i Who was the man Aladdin had met in the street?

> **Remember**
> **How to report commands**
>
> (The sorcerer to Aladdin:) 'Give the gold coins to your mother.'
>
> The sorcerer told Aladdin ***to give*** *the gold coins to* ***his*** *mother.*
>
> 'Don't lose the ring.'
>
> *He told him* ***not to lose*** *the ring.*

Writing

3 Work in small groups. Summarise the story so far. Use the answers from Exercise 2 to help you.

8.6 Aladdin: what happened next

In this lesson you will...

- listen to and write a summary of the second part of a traditional story
- use *ask*, *wonder* and the past perfect in reported speech.

- **What do you remember about the story of Aladdin so far?**

Vocabulary

58

1 **Listen to the second part of the story. Put the characters in the order of their appearance.**

a The sorcerer
b Aladdin
c The sultan's daughter
d The princess's servant
e The genie of the lamp
f Aladdin's mother *1*
g The sultan
h The genie of the ring

2 **Complete these sentences with the characters from the list in Exercise 1.**

a *Aladdin's mother* cleaned an old lamp to sell it, because they had no money.
b When she rubbed it, ... appeared and produced a table of the most wonderful food served on beautiful plates.
c One day, Aladdin saw .... and decided he wanted to marry her.
d Aladdin's mother took some treasure to ....
e Eventually, the sultan agreed that .... could marry his daughter.
f But back in Morocco, ... could not stop thinking about the lamp.
g A man in the street was shouting, 'New lamps for old,' so .... decided to take a lamp from Aladdin's room to exchange it for a new one.
h Aladdin accidentally rubbed the ring that the sorcerer had given him and .... appeared.

3 **Listen to the story again and answer the questions.**

a How did the genie of the lamp help Aladdin's mother?
b Why did Aladdin's mother go to see the sultan? What was the result?
c How did the sorcerer get the lamp from the palace and what did he do with it?
d What happened when the sultan realised that his daughter had disappeared?
e How did Aladdin help the princess escape from the sorcerer?

Use of English Reported speech: questions and statements

You can use the verb *ask* to report questions.

'**Can** you bring us some good things to eat?' Aladdin **asked** the genie.

Remember to change the tense.

*Aladdin **asked** the genie if he **could** bring them some good things to eat.*

'**Shall** I take this old lamp to the market to sell it?' **asked** Aladdin.

*Aladdin **asked** if he **should** take the old lamp to the market to sell it.*

'Where **is** my daughter? the sultan **asked** Aladdin.

*The sultan **asked** Aladdin where his daughter **was**.*

To report statements, change the present perfect to the past perfect:

'I'**ve** just **seen** the princess,' Aladdin said.

*Aladdin said that he **had** just **seen** the princess.*

You can use the verb *wonder* to report statements that begin 'I wonder ...':

'I wonder what **has happened** to the lamp?'

*The sorcerer **wondered** what **had happened** to the lamp.*

4 Report the following questions and statements. Remember to change the pronouns as well as the tenses.

a 'I've never heard anything so ridiculous,' his mother replied.
His mother replied that she had never heard anything so ridiculous.

b 'Will you allow your daughter to marry my son?' Aladdin's mother asked the sultan.
Aladdin's mother asked the sultan if he ....

c 'I've had an idea about how to get the lamp back,' the sorcerer said.
The sorcerer said he ....

d 'I wonder if I can exchange the old lamp in my master's room for a new one,' the princess's servant thought.
The princess's servant wondered if ....

e 'How can I escape from the sorcerer?' the princess asked Aladdin.
The princess ....

Writing

5 Work in groups. Write a summary of the second part of the story.

- Use your answers to Exercises 2, 3 and 4 to help you.
- Add any more details that you can remember.
- Try to include these expressions from the story:

She / He could not believe her / his eyes.
Your wish is my command.
As quick as a flash ...
New lamps for old.
She jumped for joy.
And they lived happily ever after.

8.7 Improve your writing

In this lesson you will...

- write a short essay giving your opinions about what makes a good story.

1 **An essay is organised in paragraphs. Look at the essay on the opposite page. Imagine that there were no paragraphs – in other words, imagine that it was just one long piece of text. Would it be easier or more difficult to read? Why?**

2 **Here are some phrases that you will find useful in writing an essay. Put them with the correct headings in the table.**

like	although	for example / to give an example
finally	however	a good example of this is
such as	my view is	first of all / firstly
to conclude	in summary	some people think
in conclusion	I think (that)	on the other hand
in my opinion	I believe (that)	

Introducing your own and other people's opinions	Connectors to show the sequence of your argument	Introducing examples	Showing contrast
I think (that)	*first of all / firstly*	*like*	*although*

3 **Organise your ideas before you start writing. Answer these questions.**

a What must a good story have? (Think of the plot, the characters, etc.)

b Which story would you give as an example of a good story and why?

c Which story would you give as an example of a different kind of story? (Think of one that other people might like.)

d How would you sum up the key ingredients of a good story?

4 **Read the model text below. Which of these opinions are expressed or implied in the essay?**

- **a** A reader should be able to guess how the story will end.
- **b** An author's style is important for readers.
- **c** A book you enjoyed as a child can be just as enjoyable when you read it again.
- **d** Bad characters add interest to a story.
- **e** The writer reads more mystery stories than real-life stories.
- **f** The writer enjoys poetry and non-fiction as well as fiction.

5 **Plan your essay. Use the model text to help you.**

Remember to read through your essay two or three times to check your punctuation and spelling.

Make sure your essay answers the question.

What makes a good story?

First of all, I think that a good story must have an exciting and unpredictable plot. It should have interesting characters and it should be well written, so that it's easy and enjoyable to read.

Introduce the main points of your argument.

Give more detailed opinions.

I like stories that contain mystery, suspense and surprises. In my opinion, the characters and events don't have to be realistic because a story can take you into a world of imagination.

One of my favourite books when I was younger was *Peter Pan*. I've just read it again and it is full of amazing and amusing characters, such as the evil villain, Captain Hook, who is a bad-tempered pirate, and a vindictive crocodile that has swallowed a clock. It's full of action and it's also very funny.

Give examples to back up your opinions.

Add contrasting ideas.

However, I realise that some people prefer stories that are more realistic; stories that are based on real events from history and true-life stories.

In conclusion, my view is that good stories contain similar qualities: they are exciting and imaginative and they are never disappointing.

Summarise your views.

8.8 Project challenge

Project: Aladdin – the play

You are going to write and perform a play based on the story of Aladdin.

There are eight characters: Aladdin, Aladdin's mother, the sorcerer, the genie of the ring, the genie of the lamp, the sultan, the princess and the princess's servant.

There are six scenes in the play.

1 Work in six groups. Each group writes one scene from the play, using the script outline on the opposite page.

The dialogue for the start and the end of each scene is given in the outline. You need to write the dialogue for the rest of the scene. This is shown in *blue* in the outline. Look back at Lessons 8.5 and 8.6 to help you.

Your teacher will check your script.

2 You will need the following props:

3 You are going to perform the scene you've written. Choose the parts you're going to play. If necessary, bring in students from other groups.

4 Rehearse your scene. Speak clearly and slowly and use movement and facial expressions to help the audience understand what you are saying. Your teacher will check your pronunciation.

5 Give a performance of *Aladdin*.

- Which was the most challenging part of this project and which was the most enjoyable?
- How has this project helped you to improve your English?

Describe where the scene takes place.

Scene 1 *China. Aladdin's house and the street outside.*

List the characters appearing in this scene.

ALADDIN, ALADDIN'S MOTHER, THE SORCERER

MOTHER: Aladdin! Where are you? You never help me in the house. You play with your friends all day …

ALADDIN: Bye, Mum! See you later!

Give stage directions.

Exit Aladdin.

[The sorcerer finds Aladdin, tells him he is his uncle, and promises him that he can become rich. But first Aladdin must help him …]

SORCERER: Come with me, Aladdin!

Scene 2 *China. In a beautiful garden.*

THE SORCERER, ALADDIN, THE GENIE OF THE RING

SORCERER: Now, Aladdin, you must lift this big stone and go into the cave.

[The sorcerer tells Aladdin what is in the cave: wonderful treasure … but also a lamp. He wants Aladdin to bring him the lamp. Aladdin is afraid, but the sorcerer gives Aladdin a ring to protect him. Aladdin goes into the cave, finds the treasure and the lamp, but he can't get out. The sorcerer gets angry and puts the stone back in front of the cave. Aladdin accidentally rubs the ring. The Genie of the Ring appears.]

GENIE: Your wish is my command! What do you want, Master?

ALADDIN: I want to get out of here!

Scene 3 *China. Aladdin's house.*

MOTHER, ALADDIN, THE GENIE OF THE LAMP

MOTHER: Aladdin! You're home at last! But where is your uncle?

[Aladdin explains that the man isn't his uncle, but a very bad man. Aladdin is hungry, but there's nothing to eat. His mother decides to clean the lamp, to sell it for some food. The Genie of the Lamp appears and brings food.]

MOTHER: This is wonderful!

Scene 4 *China. The market and the Sultan's palace.*

ALADDIN, MOTHER, THE GENIE OF THE LAMP, THE SULTAN, THE PRINCESS

ALADDIN: Mother, I've just seen the sultan's daughter. She is so beautiful. I'm in love with her. I want to marry her.

[Aladdin's mother explains that this is impossible: the Princess is rich, but they are poor. Aladdin says they can ask the Genie of the Lamp for money and jewels. He persuades his mother to take some treasure to the sultan.]

SULTAN: You may marry my daughter.

Scene 5 *China. Aladdin's palace.*

ALADDIN, THE PRINCESS, THE PRINCESS'S SERVANT, THE SORCERER, THE GENIE OF THE LAMP.

ALADDIN: You are my wife, we have a beautiful palace … we are so happy! And now I must go and see my dear mother.

PRINCESS: Give her my good wishes.

[Aladdin goes out. The sorcerer arrives at Aladdin's palace. 'New lamps for old,' he cries. The princess's servant gives him the magic lamp. The sorcerer makes the Genie of the Lamp appear.]

SORCERER: Take the princess, the palace and me to Morocco!

Scene 6 *Morocco. Aladdin's palace. China.*

THE PRINCESS, THE SORCERER, ALADDIN, THE GENIE OF THE RING, THE GENIE OF THE LAMP.

PRINCESS: Where am I?

[Suddenly, the princess and her palace are in Morocco! Meanwhile, in China, Aladdin comes home to find his palace has disappeared. He asks the Genie of the Ring to help him. The Genie takes Aladdin to Morocco. Aladdin gives the princess some poison to put in the sorcerer's drink. The sorcerer drinks the poison and dies. Aladdin appears. He asks the Genie of the Lamp to take him and the princess back to China.]

THE GENIES: And they all lived happily ever after!

8.9 Fiction

Traditional stories from Australia

The story on these pages is from a collection of stories originally told by Aboriginal storytellers. The stories are passed down from generation to generation. Sometimes they are accompanied by music and song; sometimes they are dramatised, so that they are presented as plays.

an emu

59

1 Read and listen to the first part of the story. Where do you think the storyteller got the idea from?

2 Work in groups. Discuss these questions.

a How does the storyteller hold your attention? (Think about the descriptions, repetition and humour.)

b What do you think is going to happen? Write down your thoughts.

Tidalick

Greedy Tidalick drinks all the water throughout the land, causing a great drought, which the creatures of Australia try to reverse.

When the world was young, Tidalick, the little frog, became very thirsty. He began to drink all the water in his waterhole. But his thirst was not quenched, and he soon found more water in a nearby river and drank and drank and drank.

Tidalick soon drank all the water that was in the river and he *grew* and *grew* and *grew*, *larger* and *larger*, as he continued to drink all the water throughout the land.

He drank the streams and then the rivers, the billabongs, lagoons, waterholes and all the waterways. It was not long before all the water was in Tidalick's enormous stomach and the land became parched and dry.

A great drought spread throughout the land. All the creatures, both of the land and of the water, suffered a terrible thirst. Trees withered, the land dried and cracked, and all the creatures suffered.

When they found out that the drought was caused by the greed of Tidalick, the giant frog, the creatures held a meeting to decide how to get Tidalick to open his mouth and share some of the water.

It was agreed that a group should go to Tidalick the greedy frog and ask him to share some of the water with others. The Kangaroo, Dingo, Goanna and Emu went together to see Tidalick. They asked him if he would open his mouth and share the water, as everyone was so very thirsty.

But Tidalick refused. He tightly closed his mouth, and not a drop of water came out.

The creatures held another meeting to discuss how they could get Tidalick to open his mouth so the water could come out. It was decided that if they could make Tidalick laugh, then the water would escape.

So all the different creatures from throughout the land gathered to where Tidalick, the giant frog, sat bloated and full of all the water from throughout the land. A procession of kangaroos jumped in line, one after the other, followed by incredible leaps and bounds that had all the animals opening their mouths in amazement and wonder. They played leap the frog, and all the creatures laughed.

Not Tidalick! He just sat there. Not a smile, not a grin, and not one drop of water left his mouth.

The next creatures to try were the tall emus, with their long legs and long necks. When they danced in formation in front of Tidalick, their dance routines had all the animals opening their mouths in amazement and wonder. One emu got all tangled up and tripped over his legs, and all the creatures laughed.

But not Tidalick! He just sat there. Not a smile, not a grin, and not one drop of water left his mouth.

Next came the wobbly wombats. With their short legs and fat, round bodies, they wobbled, one after the other, from side to side, in a long line, quick wobbles and slow wobbles, that had all the animals opening their mouths in amazement and wonder. Then one wombat wobbled the wrong way, and all the creatures laughed.

But not Tidalick! He just sat there. Not a smile, not a grin, and not one drop of water left his mouth.

The next creature to try was the kookaburra. He knew so many great jokes that even he laughed out loud.

But not Tidalick! He just sat there. Not a smile, not a grin, and not one drop of water left his mouth.

In the audience was an eel, who had lost his watery home to Tidalick, the greedy frog. The eel became so upset and angry that Tidalick would not share the water and give back his home that he slithered in front of Tidalick and began to tell him off. So upset was the eel that he became all twisted and knotted up. He looked so funny!

a goanna

1 greedy: wanting a lot more (food, money) than you need

8 his thirst was not quenched: he was still thirsty

16 billabong: (Australian) a pool of water

16 lagoon: a small lake

16 waterhole: a place where animals go to drink

19 parched: very dry

21 drought: a long period when there is no rain and therefore no water

24 wither: to become dry and start to die

48 bloated: so full that you look or feel much bigger than normal

52 leaps and bounds: small and big jumps

54 leap the frog: (or 'leap frog') a game where one person bends down and another jumps over them

65 tangled up: twisted together

72 wobble: to move unsteadily from side to side (*adjective: wobbly; noun: wobble*)

87 eel: a long thin fish that looks like a snake

91 slither: to slide along the ground like a snake

94 knotted up: tied in knots

a dingo

60

3 **Read and listen to the conclusion of the story. Did you guess how it would end?**

Suddenly, Tidalick grinned.

He smiled a big smile. Then he started to titter. You see, Tidalick had never seen an eel so angry and twisted and all knotted up before. It looked so funny he began to laugh.

His laughter quickly became a big belly laugh and, before long, the water began gushing out of Tidalick's mouth, filling the streams, rivers, billabongs, lagoons, waterholes and all the waterways across the land.

Eel was so happy that his home was back that he unknotted himself and quickly slithered right back into his watery habitat.

Tidalick became smaller and smaller, as gallons of water poured out of him, until finally he became the size that frogs are today.

The animals decided that Tidalick would never again be allowed to cause another great drought through his greed as he did in the First Time, when the world was young.

Retold with permission by Pauline E. McLeod

[3] titter: to laugh quietly, trying to stop yourself from laughing out loud

[8] belly laugh: a deep laugh

[9] gush out: to pour out suddenly and quickly

4 **Look back to the list of adjectives you can use to describe stories in Lesson 8.1. Which ones would you use to describe this story?**

Writing

5 **Work in groups. Write your own animal story by following these instructions:**

- Agree on what happens in the story.
- Write down your answers to these questions:
  - How does it begin?
  - Are there any actions that are repeated?
  - Are there any funny (humorous, comic) moments in the story?
  - What is the most dramatic part of the story?
  - How does it end?
- Write a plan of the story.
- Decide who will write each part of the story.
- Write the story.
- Read your part of the story out loud. Other members ask questions and make suggestions for changes and corrections.
- Write a final version of your story.

Check your progress

General knowledge quiz

How much can you remember about what you have learned?

1 What is a *kora* and what is its connection with storytelling?

2 A *zajal* is a poetic battle. How many people take part and in which language do the contestants speak?

3 What kind of puppets does this picture show?

4 How many people speak in a monologue?

5 In which language were the stories in *One Thousand and One Nights* originally written?

6 In which two countries is the story of Aladdin set?

7 In the story of Aladdin, who does the sorcerer pretend to be?

8 How does Aladdin make the genie of the ring appear?

9 Who is the villain in the children's story *Peter Pan*?

10 What is the missing word in this traditional final sentence of a folk tale or fairy story: 'And they all lived .... ever after'?

Vocabulary

1 **Match the types of books to the descriptions.**

a crime fiction	1 Set in 12th-century China, this story follows the life of the Emperor's daughter.
b historical fiction	2 Detective Dominic Reeves is called in when a famous work of art disappears from a museum.
c horror stories	3 Teenage astronomy enthusiasts track unusual space travel and discover a colony from Mars in Arizona.
d science fiction ('sci-fi')	4 Nightmares come to life in this account of strange night-time events and unearthly creatures.

2 **Complete each sentence with the most appropriate adjective.**

imaginative disappointing scary
amusing mysterious complicated

a The story made everyone laugh. It was very ....

b I couldn't understand what was happening in that crime series. The plot was too ....

c Sam was an .... child. He used to make up plays which were performed by his teddy bears.

d The film wasn't as good as the book. I found it rather ....

e Nobody knew the man who helped in the rescue. He was quite ....

f It's best not to watch or read anything too .... before you go to bed if you want to have a good night's sleep.

3 How good are you at explaining the meaning of words? Write a definition of each of the following words.

a author

An author is someone who writes books.

b storyteller

c puppeteer

d comedian

e translator

Use of English

1 Use the present perfect continuous to complete this conversation.

Maira: Hi, Aisha. How are you? What *you / do* today?

What have you been doing today?

Aisha: I'm fine. *I / read* a story for homework. What about you?

Maira: Oh, *I / look* after my brother and sister.

Aisha: How's it going?

Maira: Well, *we / play* a lot of football in the garden and *they / make* so much noise that now I'm feeling absolutely exhausted.

Aisha: Oh dear.

Maira: It's OK now. *They / play* a video game quite happily for the last half an hour and *they / not / fight* at all.

2 Report the following questions and answers.

a 'Have you seen a man on a black motorbike?' the detective asked Kieran.

The detective asked Kieran if he had seen a man on a black motorbike.

b 'Why is he asking me?' wondered Kieran.

c 'I've received a phone call about an incident,' the detective said.

d 'What has happened?' Kieran asked.

e 'I can't tell you,' replied the detective.

f 'Shall I contact you if I see the man again?' asked Kieran.

g 'That will be helpful,' said the detective.

Summary checklist

I can

- ☐ discuss storytelling traditions from around the world.
- ☐ talk about the stories I enjoyed when I was younger.
- ☐ read and then write a summary of a classic story.
- ☐ write a short essay giving my opinions.
- ☐ work collaboratively to write and perform a scene from a play.
- ☐ read a traditional story from Australia and answer questions about it.

9 Music

In this unit you will...

- **talk** about genres of music
- **read** about the winner of a 'Young Musician' competition
- **find out** about how music can contribute to people's lives
- **give** your opinions about three pieces of music
- **give** your own views on music as a universal language
- **interpret** some epigrams about music
- **write** a personal account of what music means to you
- **create** a presentation of music from around the world
- **write** a script for a film, with music and sound effects
- **read** an autobiography
- **write** an autobiographical account of your first day at school.

Getting started

"What sort of music do you and your friends listen to? Do you all agree on your favourite songs and pieces of music?"

Watch this!

9.1 My kind of music

In this lesson you will...

- talk about genres of music
- identify inconsistencies in what people say.

- **Why do we listen to music?**

Speaking

61 **1** **Listen to these pieces of music. First rank them: 5 stars for the one you like best, 1 star for the one you like least. Then say which of the following genres they belong to.**

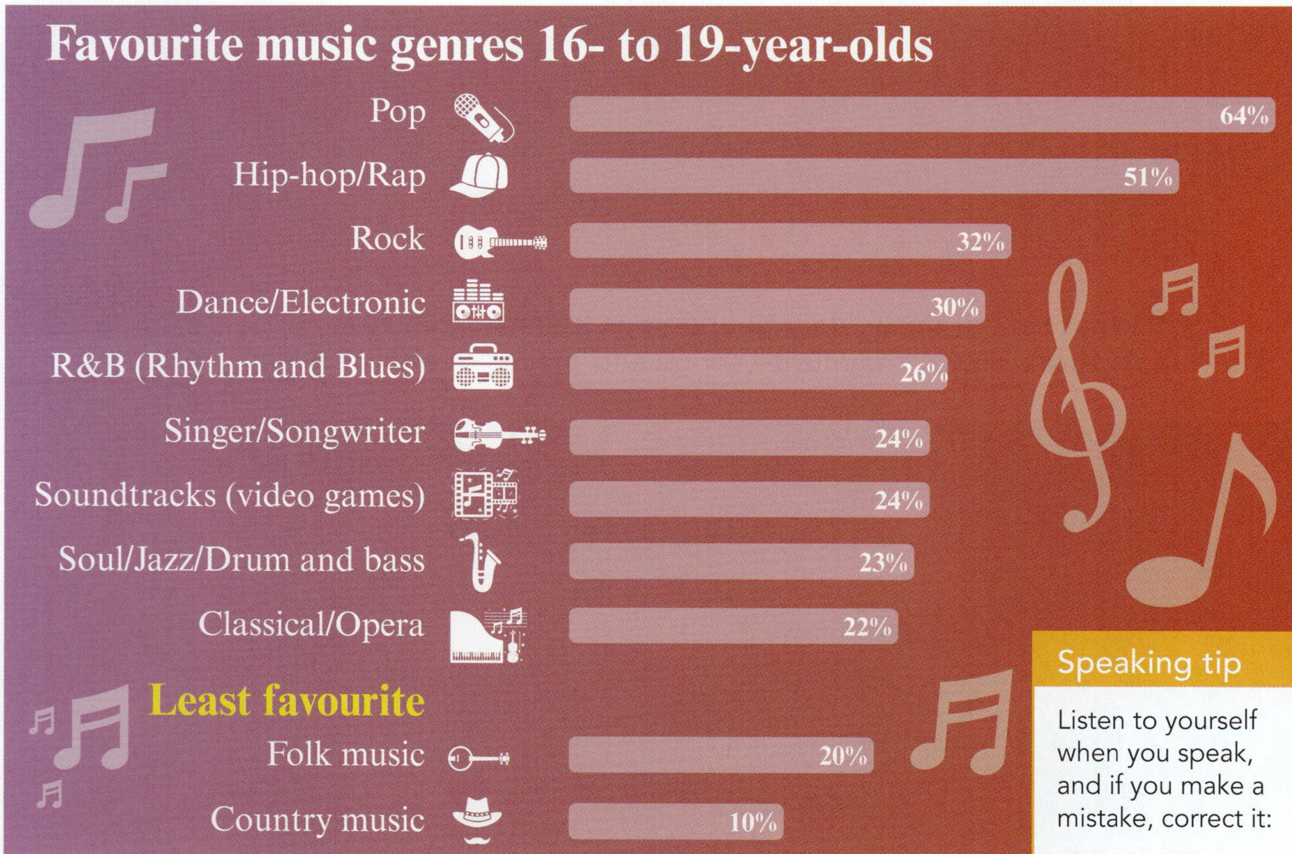

Speaking tip

Listen to yourself when you speak, and if you make a mistake, correct it:

*He's also given money for studentships – **I mean**, scholarships – at Cambridge University.*

Listening

62 **2** **Listen to these teenagers talking about music. How many genres of music do they mention?**

3 **Complete these notes and answer the questions.**

Name	Notes
Bella	Listens to [1]........ music. Not so keen on [2]........ music.
Bruno	Likes Ed Sheeran, who plays and sings [3]........- pop music, but also [4]........ . The melodies are really [5]........ and easy to remember.
Sangita	Learning to play the [6]........ and other percussion instruments. Loves the sound of the marimba because it's so [7]........ and gentle.
Alfie	He and his [8]........ Joel listen to a lot of music together. They've been listening to some of his parents' old CDs of classic [9]........ music and dance music.
James	Likes [10]........ music. He gives the example of Stormzy, who is a singer and [11]........ .

a What example does Bella give to support what she says about the music she's not keen on?

b What does Bruno like about Ed Sheeran's lyrics?

c What does Sangita mean when she says, 'Maybe my parents knew something when they named me!'?

d Why do you think Alfie would be embarrassed if his friends caught him listening to his parents' CDs?

e Why does James give the example of Stormzy as a rapper he admires?

63

4 **Listen again to the last two speakers. There's an inconsistency in what each of them says. What are the inconsistencies? Complete these sentences:**

a First, Alfie says that .... but then he says that ....

b First, James says that .... but then he says that ....

Remember Use the correct verb tense

A pop song only lasts about four minutes. NOT A pop song ~~is only lasting~~ about four minutes.

What have you been listening to recently? NOT What ~~are you listening~~ to recently?

Speaking

5 **Discuss your musical likes and dislikes. Try to include these phrases:**

Opinions

I'm not so keen on [*classical music*]

in my opinion

that's what I like

[old pop] music just doesn't do it for me

Examples

for example

like

Additional information

By the way …

he's / she's not only …; he's / she's also …

9.2 A portrait of a musician

In this lesson you will...

- read about the winner of a 'Young Musician' competition
- talk about what it means to be a professional musician.

- **Who is the best musician you can think of?**

Reading

1 **Read the extract. What is the writer's opinion of Sheku?**

Sheku Kanneh-Mason

'Just playing beautifully is kind of boring. I want to play with as much character as possible.'

He's the son of parents from Antigua and Sierra Leone, and grew up in Nottingham with six siblings, each of them a strikingly gifted musician in their own right. They appeared on *Britain's Got Talent* in 2015 – not an obvious career move for a young classical musician. Then Sheku won the 2016 BBC Young Musician competition, played at the wedding of the Duke and Duchess of Sussex in May 2018, and saw his debut recording – of Shostakovich's First Cello Concerto – climb to Number One in the US Billboard Emerging Artists chart. I'll repeat that: this is the cellist who, in 2018, took Shostakovich to the top of the US pop charts. (He knocked the rapper Lil Baby off pole position.) And here he is, still only 20, sitting in the boardroom at the RAM [the Royal Academy of Music], having just recorded Elgar's Cello Concerto with Sir Simon Rattle and the London Symphony Orchestra.

6 **siblings:** brothers and sisters

7 **strikingly:** in a way that immediately attracts your attention

7 **gifted:** having a natural ability to do something really well

14 **debut:** first public appearance

21 **pole position:** the front position at the start of a car race

22 **boardroom:** the room where the directors of a company have meetings

Speaking

2 **Work with a partner. Use the information in the extract in Exercise 1 to ask and answer questions about Sheku.**

A: ***Where is he from?***

Reading

3 Read the second extract. What impression do you get of Sheku?

'I mean, it definitely wasn't our parents' plan for all of us to play,' he explains. 'They just really loved music, so they gave us the opportunity to have lessons and we all really enjoyed it. We had a piano in the house and Isata started having lessons, and I guess we all saw her doing that and followed after. But it was never like we had to. I played lots of piano trios with my sister and brother – there's so much amazing repertoire, and you learn so much from playing in small ensembles that you certainly don't get from solo playing. That intense level of listening, and being spontaneous and responding to what someone else says in an intimate way. I love that. And you learn from each other's playing as well. It's always special playing with people you know really, really well.'

11 **repertoire:** all the songs, plays, etc. that someone can perform

13 **ensembles:** small groups of musicians or actors who regularly play or perform together

14 **intense:** having a very strong effect

15 **spontaneous:** happening naturally and suddenly and without being planned

17 **intimate:** close, friendly

4 Read the second extract again. Which phrase or sentence implies the following?

- **a** Isata is the oldest of the children.
- **b** Sheku's parents didn't force him and his brothers and sisters to practise.
- **c** He likes being creative with his playing.
- **d** Playing in groups can be more interesting than playing alone.

Key words: Music

English uses quite a few words from other languages to describe music. What do these words mean?

trio, solo (from Italian)

repertoire, ensemble (from French)

9.3 Express yourself!

In this lesson you will...

- find out about how music can improve people's lives
- talk about the value of music in education.

- **How can playing a musical instrument or singing help people in their everyday lives?**

Reading

1 **Read what this music teacher says about her work. How does she feel about it?**

I work with young people who have learning disabilities and physical disabilities. I use a group of several interactive computer programs called iMUSE, which provide a multisensory experience – an experience that involves more than one of the senses. This is how it works:

- One computer program picks up the movements a student makes and turns the movements into sounds. The student can choose which instrument to play from 126 possibilities – for example, a piano or a guitar – and make the sound of that instrument by moving part of their body.
- Another program uses sounds and turns them into beautiful, colourful images on a screen. The images change as the sounds change. The student can speak, sing or make noises into the microphone.

Each iMUSE session lasts for 30 minutes. As a teacher, you find out which sounds, music and visuals help each young person to relax and focus. Every iMUSE session is different, depending on what each student likes or dislikes.

Young people with disabilities really benefit from regular iMUSE sessions. What I've noticed is that iMUSE helps them to:

- become relaxed and calm
- make choices
- express themselves even when they are not able to speak
- concentrate and be better prepared to do other activities.

2 **Answer these questions.**

a iMUSE provides a 'multisensory experience'. Which senses are involved? What else is involved?

b What is the role of the teacher?

c How do you think students feel about their iMUSE sessions?

Listening

64 **3** **Listen to another music teacher. He's talking about his work at 'My Music'. How can making music help young people?**

4 **Answer these questions about what you have just heard.**

- **a** Why might writing the words for a song help a young person?
- **b** How do you think music might help students with other subjects?
- **c** This teacher compares sport and music. What are the similarities and differences?

'I used to try to copy the voices of other singers, but now I've found my own voice.'

'I was always very shy, but now I can get up on stage and perform in front of people. Wow! What a difference!'

'I always wanted to impress other people. I would change myself to be like them. Now, when I make music, I can be myself.'

Speaking

65 **5** **Work in groups. Discuss what the two teachers in Exercises 1 and 3 said about the value of music in education.**
To help you, you can listen to a group of students having this discussion.

What do you think of iMUSE?

Do you think making music is good for you?

- Try to include some of the structures with *what* from the Use of English box.

Speaking and writing tip

The verb *make* occurs in a lot of phrases in English. Make a note of some to use when you are speaking or writing.

We enjoy ***making music*** *together.*

It ***makes them feel*** *happier.*

It helps them ***make choices****.*

It ***makes*** *a difference.*

Use of English
what (= 'the thing(s) which')

You already know how to ask questions beginning with '*What …?*'

In the following sentences, *what* means 'the thing(s) which'.

Every session is different, depending on ***what*** *each person likes or dislikes.*

What *I've noticed is that iMUSE helps them.*

They feel proud of ***what*** *they do.*

Remember that *What a …* is a useful way of introducing an exclamation.

What a difference!

9.4 I like it because …

In this lesson you will...

- learn and use words for musical instruments and performers
- give your opinions about three pieces of music.

- **What is your favourite instrument and who is your favourite performer?**

Vocabulary

1 **Look at the words in the box. Can you add any names of instruments or performers?**

Types of music	Musical instruments	Performers
instrumental music	percussion	percussionist
orchestral music	guitar	guitarist
vocal music	piano	pianist
choral music	drums	drummer
	sitar	…

Listening and speaking

66

2 **Listen to these students in a music class. What has their teacher asked them to do?**

3 **Listen again. As you listen, note down one or two opinions that you agree with about each piece of music.**

4 **Work in groups. Compare what you have written down. Did you agree?**

Use of English Participle clauses

Participle clauses are similar to relative clauses. They're often used in conversation.

*There's **someone playing** a stringed instrument at the beginning.*	There's **someone who is playing** …
*It's like **something moving** very fast.*	It's like **something that is moving**.
*It's like **an insect flying around**.*	It's like an insect **that is flying around**.

Speaking tip

You can use *So* … to express agreement or to add to what has been said.

Notice the word order:
So do I NOT ~~*So I do*~~.

***I think** it goes on too long.*
*So **do I**.*

***I liked** it*
*So **did I**.*

***I'd** give it 9.*
*So **would I**.*

67

5 Now listen to these three pieces of music and discuss them.

- First discuss each one separately.
- Then compare them.
- Use the questions and phrases below to help you.
- Try to include participle clauses like the ones in the Use of English box.

What sort of piece is it?	It's an orchestral piece. It's a piece for solo guitar. It's about … minutes long.
What do you think of it?	It makes you feel … • calm • relaxed • sad • happy
What do you like about it?	It has … • a beautiful melody • a strong rhythm What I like is the way … That's what I like.
How would you describe the tempo (speed) of the music?	It's … • quite slow • lively
What sort of picture do you have in your mind when you listen to this?	It's like …

9.5 A universal language

In this lesson you will...

- read an article about research into music as a universal language
- give your own views on music as a universal language.

- **Do you listen to music from different countries?**

Reading

1 **Read the newspaper article. What is the 'message' of the article? Is it positive or negative?**

Music really IS a universal language

People know what type of song they are hearing, no matter where they are from.

- **A Harvard-led study asked 750 internet users from 60 different countries to listen to 14-second extracts from songs.**
- **Participants were asked to answer questions about the function of a song. Was it used 1) for dancing, 2) to express love, 3) to soothe a crying baby, 4) to heal an illness, 5) to mourn the dead, or 6) to tell a story?**

After participants had listened to more than 26,000 extracts, the data was collected and analysed. The results showed that across cultures, participants gave an accurate description of the function of a song.

Manvir Singh, one of the study's co-authors, said: 'We show that our shared psychology produces fundamental patterns in song that transcend our profound culture differences. This suggests that our emotional and behavioural responses [to songs] are remarkably similar across widely diverging populations.'

This was surprising to the researchers because most people believe that music is shaped by culture.

We know that in the animal world there are links between form and function in the sound an animal makes. When a lion roars or an eagle screeches for instance, it sounds hostile to us. But it wasn't clear, until now, whether the same was true for human song.

Psychologist Dr Samuel Mehr, co-author of the study, said that our common human nature is what makes music universal.

2 **Match the meanings to the words in the statistics key words box.**

- a someone who takes part in an activity with other people
- b a piece of work that examines a subject in detail in order to find new information
- c someone who studies a subject in order to find new information about it
- d to look at and think about something carefully in order to understand it
- e information or facts about something

Key words: Statistics

a participant
a researcher
a study
data
to analyse

3 **With a partner, find these words in the newspaper article and work out their meaning from the context.**

- a function
- b to soothe
- c to mourn
- d to transcend
- e diverging

4 **Answer these questions.**

- a The research was done at a well-known university. What is its name?
- b How was the research done? Was it done by getting all the people together?
- c How long were the extracts the participants listened to?
- d Look at what Manvir Singh says. Can you say the same thing in simpler language?
- e Look again at the title of the article. Why do you think the writer chose to put the word IS in capital letters?

Speaking

5 **Work in groups. Discuss the question 'Is music a universal language?'**

I think it is. When I listen to music from another culture, I can feel whether it's happy or sad.

I'm not so sure. When I listen to some music, I just can't understand it. For example, …

Maybe it's only true for songs.

Writing

6 **Write a response to the newspaper article for the comments section of the newspaper's website.**

I found this article interesting …

› 9.6 You are what you listen to

In this lesson you will…

- interpret some epigrams about music
- ask questions in a way that makes them sound polite.

An epigram is a short sentence that expresses something in an interesting or amusing way.

- **Can you tell what someone is like from the music they like?**

68

1 **Listen to this conversation between Raina and Tom. What do they say about the meanings of the first two epigrams?**

2 **Answer these questions.**

a Why is Tom looking at these quotes?

b Who was Hans Christian Andersen?

c Why do you think Raina says, 'That's surprising'? What does she mean?

d Who was Confucius?

e Do Tom and Raina agree about the meaning of what Confucius said?

Remember

what can mean 'the thing(s) that'

*You are **what** you listen to.* = You are **the thing(s) that** you listen to.

Use of English Questions

To make a question sound more polite, you can use another question to introduce it.

What does this mean? ***Do you know*** *what this means?*

You can also use *I wonder*.

What does this mean? ***I wonder*** *what this means.*

Notice the word order:

Do you know what this means? NOT *Do you know ~~what does this mean~~?*

I wonder what this means. NOT *I wonder ~~what does this mean~~?*

When you are asking for an opinion, you can include *do you think* in your question.

*What **do you think** that means?*

3 **Rewrite questions a to d to make them sound more polite. Rewrite question e to show that you are asking for an opinion.**

a When do we get the results of our music exam? ***Do you know …?***

b What time does the concert start? ***Do you know …?***

c How long does the concert last? ***I wonder …***

d Why do the musicians all wear black? ***I wonder …***

e What do we need for our music project? ***What do you think …?***

4 **Work in pairs or groups. Have a conversation like the one between Raina and Tom about the other quotes.**

What do you think this one means?
I suppose it means that …
You mean, …?
Do you think …?
What about …?
I wonder what it means.

9.7 Improve your writing

In this lesson you will...

- write a personal account of what music means to you.

1 **Work with a partner. Read the account on the opposite page. How does Tom answer each of the following questions?**

a What kind of music do you like?
b When do you listen to music?
c Does listening to music help you to relax, to feel calm, to concentrate? What kind of music helps you in this way?
d Where and when do you hear music in your daily life? What kind of music is it?
e When do you hear music at school?
f Why do you think music is played on important occasions?
g Is there a piece of music that is particularly memorable for you?
h Would you say that music is universal? Why?
i Do you play a musical instrument?
j Do you have any dreams or ambitions for the future connected with music? What are they?

2 **How well do you know your punctuation? Match each of the following with a number in the text.**

a Use capital letters for the titles of books and films.
b Don't use full stops after commonly used initials in abbreviations.
c , Use a comma in lists of things.
d , Use a comma after time expressions.
e : Use a colon to introduce a list.
f ; Use a semicolon to join closely connected ideas that could be separate sentences into one sentence.
g ' Use an apostrophe to show that letters are missing in a word, e.g. in the short forms of verbs.
h ' Use an apostrophe to show the possessive form of a person or thing.

3 **Write an account of what music means to you. Adapt the model text by giving your own answers to the questions in Exercise 1.**

4 **Check your writing.**

- Have you answered all the questions in Exercise 1?
- Have you checked your punctuation using the guide in Exercise 2?

What music means to me

I enjoy listening to all kinds of music. I listen to pop, rock, rap and 1 ....
electronic music. I even listen to folk and classical music, because
my parents like it, but my favourite kind of music is rap. I think it's
very expressive. I listen to music when I'm in my room at home. It
helps me to feel relaxed. If I'm reading, I usually play something with
a strong rhythm, like R&B, but when I'm doing homework, I prefer 2 ....
silence because I can concentrate better.

In daily life, you hear music everywhere: in shops, in lifts, on TV and 3 ....
in the supermarket. I don't like this kind of music; it's not what you 4 ....
want to listen to. It's just background music and often you don't
even notice it. However, when music is played for a particular reason
or on an important occasion, it is usually worth listening to because
someone has chosen it to suit the event, to make it feel special and
to help people share the experience. For example, we often have
music at a school assembly and at the end of term.

A few years ago, I went to the cinema with my parents to see the 5 ....
film of *The Hobbit*. The soundtrack was fantastic and at the end 6 ....
there was a beautiful song sung by Ed Sheeran called 'I See Fire'.
We sat in the cinema listening to the music after everyone else had
left. Ed Sheeran's voice is just amazing. It made the evening really 7 ....
memorable for me.

Music is universal because everyone can listen to it and feel what it expresses. It is a language without words. A good example of this was during the pandemic of 2020, when everyone had to stay at home. Musicians and singers entertained their neighbours by playing and singing from the windows and balconies of their apartments. It made everyone feel happier.

I've just started learning the piano. I know it's something you have 8 ....
to work at and I will have to do lots of practice, but one day, I hope
I will be able to play well enough to make people feel happy and
inspired by the music I play.

Tom Fordham

9.8 Project challenge

Project 1: A survey of favourite music genres

You're going to do a survey of favourite music genres in order to produce a poster or a digital display.

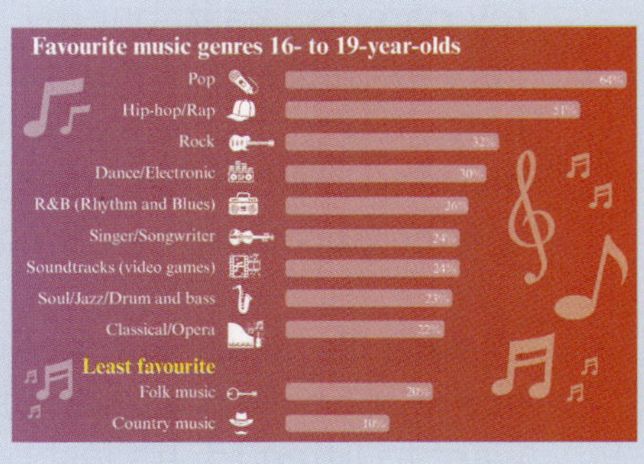

1 Look back at the chart in Lesson 9.1.

Divide the class into three or four groups. You are going to create a similar chart showing the favourite music genres of students in your class. You can either create a poster or a digital display with audio examples of each genre. Decide which you are going to do.

2 In your groups, discuss these questions:

- Should each student in the class look at the list of genres in the chart in Lesson 9.1 and write them in order of preference, starting with their favourite and ending with their least favourite? Or is there another way of finding this information?
- How will you find out about other genres – ones that are popular in your particular country, but which don't appear in the chart?
- How are you going to collect the results of your survey? Like this?

Pop

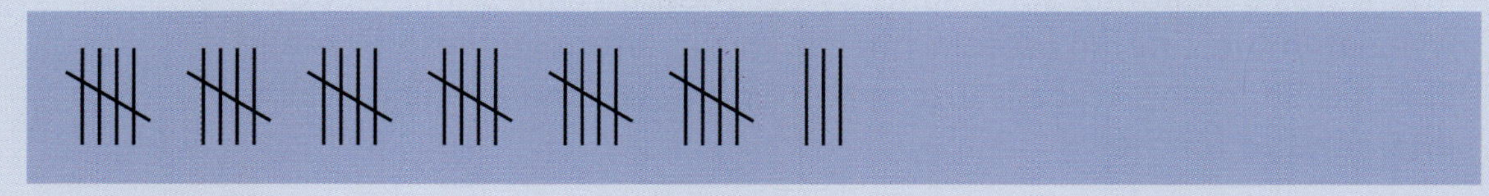

Hip-hop / Rap

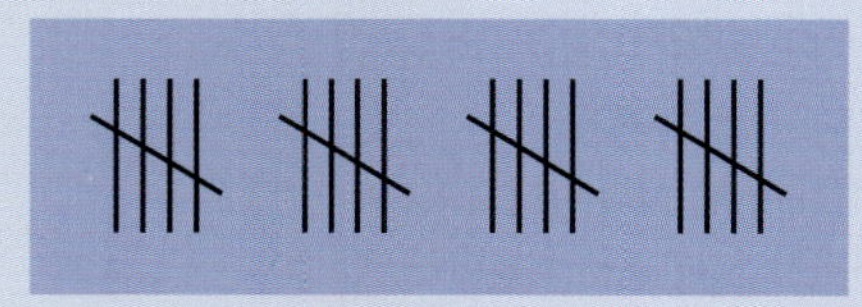

- How are you going to present the results of your survey? Like the bar chart at the top of this page? Or in another way?
- If you can illustrate your presentation with sound, how will you do this?

3 In your groups, carry out your survey and prepare your poster or digital display.

- What are the main differences between your survey and the one in Lesson 9.1?
- What would you do differently if you did this project again?

Project 2: A presentation about music

You're going to create a presentation about music from around the world.

1 Work in groups. Decide on the kind of music you are going to present. It can be one of the following or your own choice.

Andean music	Calypso music	Carnatic music
Chinese opera	Gamelan music	Flamenco

2 Find out about the music you have chosen. Write notes about each point:

- Where it comes from
- Its history
- The instruments used
- What it sounds like

Andean music is traditional folk music from Peru and Bolivia in South America.

The music includes melodies, chants and songs passed down from generation to generation by the Quechua and Aymara people living in the Andes.

The traditional instruments are flutes, panpipes, drums and horns. More recent additions are stringed instruments such as guitars, mandolins and violins.

The music is both melodic and rhythmic. It is played by South American folk groups such as Inti-Illimani and Los Incas.

melodic: has a pleasant tune

rhythmic: regular, repeating pattern of sound

3 Write one or two key sentences on each presentation slide to summarise your notes. Include a photo or illustration. Find a video or sound recording to use.

4 Give your presentation to the class. Finish with the video or sound recording.

5 Ask the class for comments and respond to any questions.

- Did the key sentences for your presentation give a clear summary of your notes? Would you change any of them if you did the presentation again?
- What did you learn from the comments and questions from the class?

9.9 Autobiography

1 Read and listen to the text. Who is Lang Lang? What is an autobiography? Why do people write autobiographies? (Audio track 69)

2 Read the text and answer the questions.

- a At the start of the extract, where is Lang Lang?
- b Who is with him?
- c What is about to happen?
- d How does he feel?
- e What is special about him?
- f What has his life been like so far?
- g How is his life about to change?

3 Work with a partner. Find these sentences in the text. Say what they mean.

- a 'She had always been able to read my mind.'
- b 'Your music will always keep you company.'
- c 'My father had long believed I was destined for greatness.'
- d 'The odds were against me.'
- e 'I had only my talent to fall back on.'

4 **clutched:** held firmly

9 **wracked:** made to suffer a lot of pain

11 **nightmares:** very frightening dreams

17 **challenging:** difficult in a way that tests your ability or determination

18 **insisted:** said very strongly

20 **eager:** very keen, wanting to do something very much

34 **prodigy:** a young person who has great natural ability

39 **dissuade:** persuade someone not to do something; *here*, make him think differently

44 **accomplished:** good at doing something that needs a lot of skill

55 **scholarship:** money given to a student by an organisation to pay for their education

67 **anticipated:** thought about in advance

Playing with Flying Keys by Lang Lang

Prologue

I was only nine years old, a third-grade student from the city of Shenyang, China, when I knew my life was going to change. I tightly clutched my mother's hand, waiting at the Shenyang station for the train to take us to Beijing, my new home. My father would be waiting for me. For the previous forty-eight hours my body had been wracked by a high fever – every bone in my body ached – and in my nightmares monsters were chasing me. When the fever finally broke, my mother pronounced me fit enough to travel and helped me pack my suitcases.

I had never been to Beijing, but I knew my life would soon be very different, harder, more challenging. I was already a gifted young pianist, but my father insisted I move to Beijing to advance my musical skills. Part of me was eager to go; another part was incredibly sad. I would miss my friends, grandparents, and teachers in Shenyang. Most of all I would miss my mother. Still holding my hand, my mother, Xiulan, looked down at me with her big brown eyes and beautiful smile. I was trying to appear brave, but she had always been able to read my mind. "Do not feel lonely or afraid, Lang Lang," she told me. "You are a very special boy. Your music will always keep you company."

In Shenyang, I had been playing the piano since before I was two, and many in my city considered me a prodigy. I had entered my first piano competition at age five. Newspapers had written stories about me and published my photo. My father had long believed I was destined for greatness, and nothing would dissuade him. But nothing would be easy either. In China in 1991, a nine-year-old pianist had little hope for a career without attending the Beijing Conservatory and learning from the country's most accomplished teachers. This was my father's dream for me, and it had become mine as well.

Admission to the conservatory was extremely competitive. Everyone had to play his or her best work for the judges. There were also written exams. I would be competing against three thousand boys and girls my age from all over China. Only fifteen in my grade would be chosen for the conservatory and to win a financial scholarship, a necessity for my family, I would have to be in the top eight.

The odds were against me. Since my father had quit his job to be with me, my family was poor and lacked influence in the world of music. My piano teacher since I was four, a woman named Professor Zhu, did not have the power of teachers from bigger cities. To those at the conservatory, whose authority and power would determine my future, I was practically invisible. But my father, a clever man, had anticipated all this. To make up for our disadvantages, he had ordered me to practise with incredible discipline since I was three years old. He knew that one day I would be competing against the best and brightest in a country of more than a billion people. I had only my talent to fall back on. I had to be prepared.

4 Read and listen to the next section of the Prologue. What does the last sentence mean?

Now the moment of truth was near. Was I prepared enough for the conservatory judges? I knew my father would not tolerate failure. As the train pulled up on that grey, overcast morning and my mother and I waited for the conductor's signal to board, my blood rushed through my ears. Could I really succeed in Beijing? What if I disappointed my father? My mother reached over with her handkerchief to dab my tears.

"Your father will meet us at the train station. He has an apartment already picked out. And your piano will be waiting for you as well."

"But I want you to live with us, Mother." I couldn't stop crying.

"Lang Lang, I don't want to be separated from you either. But I need to stay at my job in Shenyang. I am our family's only breadwinner for now. Your father is sacrificing everything to get you into the conservatory. He must find you a new teacher in Beijing. There is much work to be done before the entrance exam."

There was no arguing with my mother. Her mind was made up, even if her heart was divided. I saw a tear in her eye and I wanted to wipe it away. She was to accompany me to Beijing, stay for a day or two until I was comfortable, and then return to Shenyang, where she worked as a telephone operator for China Science Institute, Shenyang Quarter. I would miss her cooking, her stories, and her tenderness. My father was my motivator and disciplinarian, but my mother was my emotional anchor. I wondered how I could survive in a strange city of ten million people without her.

"Time to go," she said softly, pulling me along. "A great adventure awaits you. I know it in my heart, Lang Lang." They named me Lang Lang. In Chinese my given name, *Lang*, means "brightness and sunshine," and my family name, Lang, means "educated gentleman." Thanks to my parents for having given me such a wonderful name, I now had to live up to their expectations.

5 With a partner, ask and answer these questions.

a Who is Lang Lang going to travel with from Shenyang to Beijing?

b Where will he live, and with whom?

c Why will his mother go back to Shenyang?

d How does his mother persuade him that this is the right thing to do?

e What impression do you get of Lang Lang's mother and father?

f What are the advantages and disadvantages of being a child prodigy?

Creative writing

6 Write an autobiographical account of your first day at school. First, work in groups and discuss these questions.

- How did you feel before you went?
- What can you remember about it?
- How did you feel at the end of the day?

Start like this: ***I was … years old.***

Check your progress

General knowledge quiz

How much do you remember about what you have learned?

1 In classical music, what do we call a play with music, in which most of the words are sung?

2 Which instrument does Sheku Kanneh-Mason play? Is it:

a the violin?
b the cello?
c the piano?

3 An *ensemble* is a group of musicians playing together. *Repertoire* describes the pieces of music a performer has learned and can perform. Which language do the words *ensemble* and *repertoire* come from?

4 What is the Italian musical term for a piece for three instruments?

5 What is a 'multisensory experience'?

6 What is a *sitar*?

7 The Russian composer Rimsky-Korsakov wrote a piece that has become very famous about a flying insect. What is the insect?

8 In music, what is the word *tempo* used to describe? Is it:

a the length of a piece of music?
b the range of sound, from quiet to loud?
c the speed at which a piece is played?

9 Hans Christian Andersen said, 'Where words fail, music speaks.' But he wasn't a musician. What was he?

10 Who is Lang Lang and what is *Playing with Flying Keys*?

Vocabulary

1 **The vowels sounds (*a*, *e*, *i*, *o*, *u* and *y*) are missing from these words for music genres. Complete them.**

a d _ n c _
b h _ p – h _ p
c _ l _ c t r _ n _ c
d j _ z z
e r h _ t h m & b l _ _ s

2 **Read the text. Find the words to match the definitions below.**

My friend's cousin Amir is studying music at the Academy. I went to his end-of-term concert and it was clear as soon as he started to sing that he loves performing. He had composed some of the songs he sang – there was one I remember well. The lyrics were taken from a poem by Khalil Gibran and the melody that Amir had written was just beautiful. He accompanied himself on the guitar. He's a very gifted musician.

a playing, singing, acting for other people to enjoy
b written (a piece of music)
c words (of a song)
d tune
e talented, clever

Use of English

1 Choose the correct form of the verb in *italics* to complete this dialogue.

Lara: I'm sorry I'm late. I *am practising / have been practising*[1] since 8 o'clock this morning and I *forgot / am forgetting*[2] to look at the time!

Aunt Emily: *Are you practising / Do you practise*[3] for an exam?

Lara: No, this is for the school concert. I *had / have had*[4] my exam last Tuesday. I *haven't had / didn't have*[5] the results yet, but I *am thinking / think*[6] it went OK.

Aunt Emily: Tell me about the concert.

Lara: Well, I'm in a piano trio and in the concert we *play / are playing*[7] a mixture of classical music and more modern music.

Aunt Emily: That sounds nice. I *like / 'd like*[8] to come!

2 Complete the second sentence so that it means the same as the first.

a Do you remember the clothes you were wearing?
Do you remember what you were wearing?

b I'm pleased with the things you have done.
I'm pleased with ....

c You said something which is very interesting.
.... is very interesting.

d This is the thing I meant to show you.
This is ....

3 Combine these sentences using participle clauses. Follow the example.

a I can hear someone in the room below. That person is playing a flute.
I can hear someone playing a flute in the room below.

b Can you see me in the photo?
I'm standing next to my cousin.

c I can smell something in the kitchen.
It's burning!

d There's a bird at the window.
It's tapping!

Summary checklist

I can

- [ ] identify and talk about different genres of music.
- [ ] talk about the importance of music in people's lives.
- [ ] give opinions about pieces of music.
- [ ] discuss the question 'Is music a universal language?'
- [ ] adapt questions to make them sound more polite.
- [ ] create a poster or a digital display of favourite music genres.
- [ ] give a presentation about music from around the world.